OXFORD WORLD'S CLASSICS

ANONYMOUS *and*
WILLIAM SHAKESPEARE

Arden of Faversham

With an Introductio

IMAN SHEEH

Text edited by

TERRI BOURUS

GARY TAYLOR

OXFORD
UNIVERSITY PRESS

OXFORD
UNIVERSITY PRESS

Great Clarendon Street, Oxford, OX2 6DP,
United Kingdom

Oxford University Press is a department of the University of Oxford.
It furthers the University's objective of excellence in research, scholarship, and education by publishing worldwide. Oxford is a registered trade mark of Oxford University Press in the UK and in certain other countries.

Published in the United States of America by Oxford University Press
198 Madison Avenue, New York, NY 10016, United States of America

British Library Cataloguing in Publication Data
Data available

Library of Congress Control Number: 2025951489

ISBN 9780192872685

Printed and bound in the UK by
Clays Ltd, Elcograf S.p.A.

The manufacturer's authorized representative in the EU for product safety is Oxford University Press España S.A. of Parque Empresarial San Fernando de Henares, Avenida de Castilla, 2 – 28830 Madrid (www.oup.es/en or product.safety@oup.com). OUP España S.A. also acts as importer into Spain of products made by the manufacturer.

The manufacturer's authorised representative in the EU for product safety is Oxford University Press España S.A. of El Parque Empresarial San Fernando de Henares, Avenida de Castilla, 2 – 28830 Madrid (www.oup.es/en or product.safety@oup.com). OUP España S.A. also acts as importer into Spain of products made by the manufacturer.

OXFORD WORLD'S CLASSICS

THE NEW OXFORD SHAKESPEARE

General Editors for The New Oxford Shakespeare:
Gary Taylor, John Jowett, Terri Bourus, Gabriel Egan

General Editor for Oxford World's Classics: Emma Smith

The New Oxford Shakespeare offers authoritative editions of Shakespeare's works combining cutting-edge textual scholarship with editorial material from leading scholars in the field. Derived from the landmark *The New Oxford Shakespeare Complete Works: Modern Critical Edition*, these Oxford World's Classics editions have been designed with today's reader, student, and playgoer in mind, offering fresh interpretations of Shakespeare's plays and poems alongside comprehensive critical apparatus. New introductions provide context and criticism drawn from the latest research in the field; notes on the text detail the editorial decisions made and alternative possibilities; and the bibliography points readers to more research on specific plays, topics, and on Shakespeare Studies as a whole.

IMAN SHEEHA is a Senior Lecturer in Shakespeare and Early Modern Literature at Brunel University of London. She is the author of two books: *Household Servants in Early Modern Domestic Tragedy* (2020) and *Neighbourly Relationships in Early Modern Drama: Staged Communities* (2025).

TERRI BOURUS is Professor of Theatre and Professor of English at Florida State University. She is a General Editor of *The New Oxford Shakespeare* and the author of *Young Shakespeare's Young Hamlet* (2014). She has written essays on stage directions, the performance of religious conversion, Shakespeare and Fletcher's *Cardenio*, the role of Alice in *Arden of Faversham*, and Middleton's female roles. Bourus is an Equity actor, and has directed and acted in two very different productions of *Hamlet*, both based on Q1.

GARY TAYLOR is Robert O. Lawton Distinguished Professor at Florida State University. He is a General Editor of *The New Oxford Shakespeare* and has written, edited, and co-edited numerous other volumes including *Reinventing Shakespeare* (1989), *The Oxford Handbook of Thomas Middleton* (2012), and *Textual Genealogies and Shakespeare's History Plays* (2025). He general-edited the *Signs of Race* and *History of Text Technologies* series, founded the interdisciplinary History of Text Technologies programme at FSU in 2006, and has written about the practice and theory of editing in various periods and genres.

THE NEW OXFORD SHAKESPEARE

All's Well That Ends Well
Anthony and Cleopatra
Arden of Faversham
As You Like It
The Comedy of Errors
Coriolanus
Cymbeline
Hamlet
Henry IV, Part I
Henry IV, Part II
Henry V
Henry VI, Part I
Henry VI, Part II
Henry VI, Part III
Julius Caesar
King Henry VIII / All Is True
King John
King Lear
Love's Labour's Lost
Macbeth
Measure for Measure
The Merchant of Venice
The Merry Wives of Windsor
A Midsummer Night's Dream
Much Ado About Nothing
Narrative Poems
Othello
Pericles
Richard II
Richard III
Romeo and Juliet
Sonnets
The Taming of the Shrew
The Tempest
The Two Gentlemen of Verona
The Two Noble Kinsmen
Timon of Athens
Titus Andronicus
Troilus and Cressida
Twelfth Night
The Winter's Tale

PREFACE

Why read a new Shakespeare edition? Why read this one?

The answer to this question is paradoxical. In part it draws on Shakespeare's perennial interest or timelessness, and in part on the opposite, timeliness: the changing understanding of how his texts might operate in their own world and ours.

Shakespeare's perennial interest is a familiar enough concept. Since Ben Jonson's prescient comment about his friend and rival as 'not of an age but for all time' in the prefatory poem to the first collected edition of the plays in 1623, we have been used to recognizing Shakespeare's genius as a version of longevity. If, as Italo Calvino suggested, a classic is 'a book which has never exhausted all it has to say to its readers', Shakespeare is indefatigable.

But part of this timelessness is actually a serial topicality. Shakespeare is timely because his works continue to speak to issues of identity, politics, and culture in new ways. 'Cross-dressing' characters read differently as ideas around binary gender shift; the green world of the comedies strikes a different note in a climate emergency; mobs on stage echo with fears about the energies of populism. The plays often capture a significant moment in the consolidation of certain cultural fictions—about racial difference, for instance, or about the place of the individual in a larger historical frame. The new introductions to this edition are attentive to the ways Shakespeare is meaningful right now, as well as across time.

Alongside these new interpretative resonances are, literally, new texts. The history of editing Shakespeare's works has been shaped by assumptions about him. Was he an inspired poet who really disdained his popular audiences and their demands, as earlier editors used to suggest? Or was he passionate about theatre as a genre in which the author is only one agent of meaning, and in which bringing the work to life involves a collaborative team including actors, musicians, stagehands, and audiences? The inspired poet model tends to produce tidy texts emphasizing linguistic fluency and singular authorship; the theatrical model is more interested in the idea that Shakespeare worked with other writers and that his works were themselves dynamic scripts rather than static literary monuments. According to this latter logic, then, all versions of a play in print are provisional, of their time. And so too are the ones printed in this series.

Emma Smith

CONTENTS

GENERAL EDITORS' PREFACE TO *THE NEW OXFORD SHAKESPEARE*

The Oxford World's Classics Shakespeare is based upon the texts and commentaries of *The New Oxford Shakespeare: Complete Works*. That edition was produced by an international multigenerational team, using new research tools and methods to investigate systematically several interrelated historical and textual questions. What did Shakespeare write? When did he write it? Which of his works were written in collaboration with other playwrights? Which of his posthumously published texts contain later revisions or additions (by himself or others)? How did the evolving infrastructure and routines of the early modern multimedia entertainment industry influence what Shakespeare wrote and how it was performed? How did the technology of early modern printing and the economics of early modern bookselling influence the texts that survive? Were specific texts censored? What do his words mean? How were they pronounced in his lifetime? How should they be spelled for modern readers? How should his sentences be punctuated for modern readers and actors? How can, or should, prose be distinguished from verse? Can we recover the original music for the songs in his plays?

The New Oxford Shakespeare offers readers more forms of his writing than any other edition. Uniquely, it contains two different printed editions of the *Complete Works*. The *Critical Reference Edition* (in original spelling and punctuation) includes textual and bibliographical introductions with comprehensive textual notes; the works are arranged in the order in which the texts were first edited, from the 1592 printing of *Arden of Faversham* to the 1727 printing of *Double Falsehood*, Lewis Theobald's adaptation of Shakespeare and Fletcher's *The History of Cardenio*. In contrast, the *Modern Critical Edition* (in modernized spelling and punctuation) introduces each work with a curated international bricolage of verbal and visual responses by scholars, critics, actors, and artists over the centuries; its commentaries focus on semantic and performance interpretation; the works are arranged in the order in which they seem to have been written, beginning with *The Two Gentlemen of Verona* (1587?) and ending with *The Two Noble Kinsmen* (1613–14). An *Authorship Companion* surveys the external and internal evidence for what Shakespeare wrote and when he wrote it. The *New Oxford Shakespeare Online* combines and links both versions of the *Complete Works* with the *Companion*, supplementing them all with linked digital images of the original documents. Finally, the *Complete Alternative Versions* brings together additional texts of those plays and poems that exist in more than one early but significantly different incarnation, ranging from the 1594 printing of *The First Part of the Contention of the Two Famous Houses of York and Lancaster* to the 1623 printing of *The Tragedy of King Lear*; again, each text in the *Critical Reference Edition* is also presented in a *Modern Critical Edition*, and all are incorporated into Oxford Scholarly Editions Online, alongside the *Complete Works.*

Every edition of Shakespeare seeks to preserve and restore the complex, radiant energies of the artistic objects he created more than four centuries ago. But in the *New Oxford Shakespeare*, each of Shakespeare's surviving works is edited from a uniquely systematic and comprehensive perspective. Moreover, unlike most editions of Shakespeare, the *New Oxford Shakespeare* is not a reprint of any previous edition. It is based on direct re-examination of the surviving original documents. But no early modern text is entirely error-free, and different copies of the same edition contain variants introduced during printing. There is no evidence that Shakespeare himself proofread any of the texts of his work printed in his own lifetime. Shakespeare's editors try to do the proofreading that Shakespeare did not.

Even when early printers accurately reproduced the manuscripts they had purchased, those manuscripts themselves may have differed, intentionally or unconsciously, from what Shakespeare originally wrote. Handwritten manuscripts, like hand-printed editions, all contain unintended mistakes. In addition, texts could not be published or performed in early modern England unless they had been read, approved, and licensed by politically appointed officials, who could remove or alter material they considered objectionable. Punishments for criticizing the monarchy (treason) or the state religion (blasphemy and treason) were severe; allusions to important persons, incitements to public disorder, or words too explicitly sexual were also likely to be censored. Just what constituted 'objectionable' varied with time and the censor's own preferences. Demonstrably, some early texts of

Shakespeare's plays were censored on political and religious grounds. And some modern editions censor Shakespeare, too, by either preferring censored texts or refusing to explain his sexual meanings. We gloss delicate sexual innuendoes delicately, but when Shakespeare used a pointedly crude or vulgar expression, our commentary supplies a crude modern equivalent.

The Oxford World's Classics Shakespeare, like the *Modern Critical Edition*, seeks to make Shakespeare as accessible as possible for contemporary readers. Almost everyone first encounters Shakespeare by reading a modernized text or hearing a modernized performance (just as every modern reader of the Bible begins with an edited text translated from several ancient languages). Our texts apply the principles for scholarly modernization of spelling developed by Sir Stanley Wells in 1979, which have been widely praised and adopted. When the original spellings are ambiguous, we record both interpretations of the word in the commentary notes. We also modernize the text by using markers (diacritics) over certain letters to clarify the rhythms of the verse. We take for granted the modern elided form of the past participle (where a word like 'charged' is a monosyllable) but add an accent to call attention to the now-obsolete two-syllable pronunciation often used by Shakespeare and his contemporaries, as in 'Shall stand sore chargèd for the wasteful vengeance' (*Henry V* 1.2.283). For the same reason, we use a diaeresis to indicate the obsolete disyllabic pronunciation of 'ion', as in 'Such beastly shameless transformatïon' (*Henry IV, Part I* 1.1.44), or 'ean', as in 'A peaceful progress to the ocëan' (*King John* 2.1.340). Likewise, when modern usage stresses a different syllable, we indicate the obsolete pronunciation with an accent, as in 'As other of such vinegar aspèct' (*Merchant of Venice* 1.1.54).

Gary Taylor, John Jowett,
Terri Bourus, and Gabriel Egan

INTRODUCTION

The Lamentable Tragedy of Master Arden of Faversham

True crime repackaged for popular consumption and framed as entertainment is not a twenty-first-century phenomenon. Sixteenth-century theatre heralded this important development in popular entertainment with its publication in 1592 of *The Tragedy of Master Arden of Faversham*, written collaboratively by Shakespeare and an anonymous playwright. Based on the murder of Thomas Arden in Faversham in 1551 by his wife Alice and her accomplices, the play depicts Alice Arden's increasingly desperate attempts to kill her husband so as to be with her lover, Mosby.[1] Enlisting the help of servants, neighbours, and mercenary murderers and being thwarted at every turn, Alice and Mosby finally manage to kill Arden in his own home while he entertains Mosby with a game of backgammon and awaits dinner. Following a quick search of the house and its surroundings, the community identifies clues to the murder, collects forensic evidence, and locates the body, triggering the arrest of Arden's murderers. An Epilogue records the punishment of most accomplices and holds Arden partially responsible for his fate. Anticipating modern true crime shows, *Arden* examines the disruption of order (domestic, social, economic) murder causes, grants its audience a sense of participation in the achievement of justice through active observation and judgement, and ends with the restoration of order in the form of punishment meted out to those who have violated it.[2]

Genre

Arden of Faversham is the earliest surviving example of a genre we now label 'domestic tragedy'.[3] Distinguishing themselves from traditional

[1] Lisa Hopkins suggests that domestic tragedies anticipate the detective story genre. See '"Crimson Snow": *Arden of Faversham* as Golden Age Detective Story', in Peter Kirwan and Duncan Salkeld (eds), *Arden of Faversham: A Critical Reader* (London: Bloomsbury, 2023), 169–89.

[2] Tanya Horeck, *Justice on Demand: True Crime in the Digital Streaming Era* (Detroit: Wayne State University Press, 2019).

[3] Titles of lost plays, such as *History of the Cruelty of a Stepmother* (1578) and *History of Murderous Michael* (1579), suggest that *Arden* may have been preceded in generic innovation (Lena Cowen Orlin, 'Domestic Tragedy: Private Life on the Public Stage', in Arthur F. Kinney (ed.), *A Companion to Renaissance Drama* (Oxford: Blackwell, 2002), 372).

tragedies, *Arden* and the domestic tragedies which followed it in the late sixteenth and early seventeenth centuries often draw attention to their novelty and generic experimentation. In the Prologues and Epilogues of these plays, playwrights signal their awareness that they were departing from a theatrical norm and offering, instead, something new and inventive. The Epilogue of *Arden of Faversham*, for example, describes it as a 'naked tragedy', lacking in 'filed points' and devoid of 'glozing stuff', that is, stylistic embellishments, which would have 'ma[d]e it gracious to the ear or eye'.[4] Similarly, at the outset of the anonymous domestic tragedy *A Warning for Fair Women*, a character impersonating 'Tragedy' appears onstage, only to be mocked by a personified 'Comedy' as 'mistress buskins with a whirligig', epithets which evoke the traditional accoutrements of classical tragedy.[5] The Epilogue of this play too registers its departure from classical tragedy: 'Perhaps it may seem strange unto you [the audience] all, | That one hath not revenged another's death | ... Bear with this true and home-borne Tragedy, | Yielding so slender argument and scope'. The absence in this play of the archetypal tragic theme, revenge (such as we see in *Hamlet*, for example), and its domestic concerns, 'home-borne', mark its difference from traditional tragedy. The Prologue of Thomas Heywood's *A Woman Killed with Kindness*, another domestic tragedy, similarly advises the audience to expect no spectacular scenes or flights of the imagination: 'Look for no glorious state, our Muse is bent | Upon a barren subject, a bare scene.'[6] The novelty and generic daring of domestic tragedies, then, consisted in their fresh re-conceptualization of tragedy as a genre.

The traditional theory of drama, with its origins in Aristotle, assigned the treatment of the domestic concerns of the non-elite to the medium of comedy, designating tragedy as the appropriate genre for the depiction of royal characters grappling with affairs of state. As Sir Philip Sidney explained, 'high and excellent Tragedy' concerns

[4] *The Tragedy of Master Arden of Faversham*, ed. M. L. Wine (London: Methuen, 1972), Epilogue, 14–18.

[5] *A Warning for Fair Women: A Critical Edition*, ed. Charles Dale Cannon (The Hague: Mouton, 1975), sig. A2^r, 19. 'Buskins' were boots worn by actors of tragedy in ancient Greece and became associated with tragedy as a genre.

[6] Thomas Heywood, *A Woman Killed with Kindness*, in Martin Wiggins (ed.), *A Woman Killed with Kindness and Other Domestic Plays* (Oxford: Oxford University Press, 2008), Prologue, 3–4.

'kings' and 'Tyrants' and 'teaches the uncertainty of this world; and upon howe weak foundations guilden [golden] roofs are built'. 'Comedy', on the other hand, is concerned with 'the common errors of our life'.[7] The conventional difference between tragedy and comedy corresponded to the difference between 'king' and 'common[er]' and their respective dwellings: 'the golden roofs' as opposed to humble homes. Characters like Master Arden of Faversham, whose title, 'Master', positions him socially among the gentry, were traditionally excluded from tragedy. The domestic problem he faces in the form of his wife's infidelity and his resultant cuckoldry further position him as a comic figure. The cuckold was a figure of ridicule in early modern culture and subject to community shaming rituals. His horns, symbolizing his cuckoldry, were imagined by scandalized neighbours as hindering his access to his own home, capturing his loss of domestic control.[8] Thus in Thomas Heywood's domestic tragedy *A Woman Killed with Kindness* (1603), a cuckolded husband experiences his wife's infidelity as rendering him a stranger in his own home. He must forge fake keys and steal into the house at night like a thief to catch her and her lover in bed. *Arden*'s novelty and generic daring are announced on its title-page: 'The Lamentable and True Tragedy of M[aster] Arden of Feversham in Kent': the elevation of a mere 'Master' to the status of tragic subject would have sounded to early modern ears as an oxymoron at this point in theatre history.[9]

Generically different and innovative as they were, domestic tragedies emerged from, and spoke to, new developments in early modern print culture as well as responding to social and cultural changes. Arden's murder, for example, like the murders dramatized in other domestic tragedies, was featured in various print forms, including a ballad, and in one of the most important sixteenth-century historical texts, Raphael Holinshed's *Chronicles of England, Scotland, and Ireland*.[10] Other murders, such as that of Master George Saunders by

[7] Philip Sidney, *An Apology for Poetrie* (written 1580s; published posthumously in 1595), sigs. $F3^r$–$F4^r$.

[8] Bernard Capp, *When Gossips Meet: Women, Family, and Neighbourhood in Early Modern England* (Oxford: Oxford University Press, 2003), 193.

[9] The spelling 'Feversham' is an alternative to 'Faversham'. Notably, as the editors observe, it also puns on the sense of fever and shame attached to the murder.

[10] The official account of the murder appeared in the Wardmote Book of Faversham. The crime was also recorded in the *Breviat Chronicle* of 1551, in the diary of Henry Machyn, a London merchant, as well as in Stow's *Annals of England* (1592, 1631).

his wife and her accomplices in 1570, found a home in the thriving genre of the murder pamphlet and ballad, both cheap, thus accessible popular forms of print, before being dramatized in the play *A Warning for Fair Women* (1599). A ballad ('The complaint and lamentation of Mistress Arden of [Fav]ersham'), written in the voice of Mistress Arden and representing her as remorseful, appeared in 1633, the year in which the third edition of the play was printed, attesting to the continuing popularity of the murder story almost a century after Arden's murder. This edition was also accompanied by a woodcut image, also featured in the ballad, depicting Master Arden's murder, thus offering an accessible version of the story to those unable to read. Playgoers would have been familiar with Arden's story from such sources, and playwrights would have been encouraged by the evident public appetite for retellings of murder stories in other cultural forms.

The genre also spoke to contemporary domestic cultural and social changes. Domestic tragedies place the non-elite household and its concerns at their heart, asserting, as literary critic Emma Whipday writes, 'the importance of the private world and show[ing] that households outside the elite sphere can be performed on stage and taken seriously'.[11] There is a reason why this proved appealing to contemporary playgoers. Early modern culture witnessed an increasing emphasis on the individual household as a crucial site of social control, training ground for obedient and industrious subjects, and the foundation for an ordered state.[12] This increased emphasis has been explained as 'the ultimate impact of the English Reformation [which] fatally weaken[ed] the role the church was able to play in the defence of order'.[13] Early modern neighbourhoods were imagined as moral communities in which the responsibility for ensuring order and harmonious coexistence resided with the members of the community. Neighbours were encouraged to keep an eye on each other's homes with a view to identifying transgression and policing disorder. As William Harrison observed in 1602: 'In England every citizen is bound by oath to keep a sharp eye at his neighbour's house, as to whether the married people

[11] Emma Whipday, *Shakespeare's Domestic Tragedies: Violence in the Early Modern Home* (Cambridge: Cambridge University Press, 2019), 16–17.

[12] Lena Cowen Orlin, *Private Matters and Public Culture in Post-Reformation England* (Ithaca, NY, and London: Cornell University Press, 1994), 17.

[13] Susan Dwyer Amussen, *An Ordered Society: Gender and Class in Early Modern England* (New York: Basil Blackwell, 1988), 23.

live in harmony.'[14] Those found engaged in transgressive behaviour, such as domineering wives or, increasingly in the seventeenth century, abusive husbands, were subjected to communal shaming rituals, known as skimmington rides, which saw the community verbally humiliating and sometimes physically abusing alleged moral offenders.[15] In this cultural climate, plays inviting audiences to examine the nature of domesticity, identify sources of household disorder, and participate, through a fantasy of communal togetherness, in the workings of justice would have been appealing.[16]

'A private matter': The Public and the Private

The private home in early modern England was understood to be linked to the public, order within as impacting order outside, and disorder within doors as potentially having consequences for the community at large. Given this cultural context, the fact that one of the earliest accounts of Master Arden's murder appeared in a historical work which was Shakespeare's source for his history plays, Holinshed's *Chronicles of England, Scotland, and Ireland* (1577, 1587), should not be surprising. Dealing with topics traditionally deemed appropriate to a work on history, the defeat of the Spanish Armada and the assassination of an anointed king, for example, Holinshed decided to halt his narrative to include an account of the murder of 'a gentleman named Arden, most cruelly murdered and slain by the procurement of his own wife'. Holinshed expresses discomfort about his decision to include this domestic and local murder in a book about national history, explaining: 'The which murder, for the horribleness thereof, although otherwise it may seem to be but a private matter, and therefore as it were impertinent to this history, I have thought good to set it forth somewhat at large.'[17] Holinshed does not clarify what he found particularly 'horrible' about the murder. Critics, however, have suggested that the 'horribleness' of the story lies in Alice's persistent pursuit and the shocking number of her accomplices.[18]

[14] Qtd Orlin, *Private Matters and Public Culture*, 7.

[15] Capp, *When Gossips Meet*, 234.

[16] Orlin, *Private Matters and Public Culture*, 8–9.

[17] Holinshed's *Chronicles of England, Scotland, and Ireland* (1587), in *The Tragedy of Master Arden of Faversham*, ed. Wine, 148.

[18] Orlin, 'Domestic Tragedy: Private Life on the Public Stage', 368.

While Holinshed seems to uphold, even as he violates, a distinction between 'public' and 'private matters', the private and the public were far from being separate spheres in the lived reality of most people in early modern England. Domesticity was not synonymous with privacy. Most early modern households, unlike their twenty-first-century counterparts, for example, included servants. Michael and Susan, the Ardens' servants, who cannot but become aware of, and implicated in, their mistress's murderous plans, register the lack of privacy in the early modern home. Capturing this fact, Terri Bourus's 2014 production at Indiana University-Purdue University, Indianapolis, brought Susan into the web of the murder plot earlier than the playwrights do: in this production, Mistress Arden addresses her soliloquy in scene 1 (97–101) directly to her maidservant, stressing the claustrophobic nature of the home and the impossibility of keeping secrets in such a public domestic space. Similarly, in Polly Findlay's 2014 production for the RSC, Susan (Elspeth Brodie), unlike her counterpart on the page, remains on stage throughout the performance, witnessing and observing the unfolding of the murder plot while she performs various cleaning tasks. This production took seriously the play's depiction of a world where the boundaries between the private and the public are blurred and where domestic disorder has public consequences. The entire action took place in Master Arden's factory, and his identities as negligent husband, greedy businessman, and uncharitable neighbour were fused.

Employers enjoyed little more privacy than their servants. '[T]he early modern household,' as social historian Laura Gowing observes, 'was not built for privacy', and masters and mistresses found themselves as much the objects of their servants' surveillance as servants themselves were the objects of their masters'.[19] Such a situation is explored in Thomas Heywood's domestic tragedy *A Woman Killed with Kindness* (1603), where an unfaithful wife becomes subject to her servant's suspicions and eventual revelation of the affair to his master. This relative lack of privacy was magnified by social practice: even in elite families, servants often slept in the same rooms with their

[19] Laura Gowing, *Domestic Dangers: Women, Words, and Sex in Early Modern London* (Oxford: Oxford University Press, 1998), 190.

masters and mistresses.[20] The fact that Mistress Arden grants the painter, Clarke, access to Susan, her maidservant ('Go to her, Clarke; she's all alone within' (1.542)) without the latter's consent is a case in point. As a servant rendered vulnerable by virtue of both her gender and social status, Susan does not have the right to bodily or spatial control.[21] The Richmond Shakespeare Society 2024 production at The Mary Wallace Theatre cast a woman of colour, Vinutha Hedge, as Susan, adding a further layer of intersection to her identity. This Susan pleaded desperately with her mistress not to marry her off to Clarke (Rebecca Fallon) while the white Alice (Fleur de Henrie Pearce) sat unresponsive and looking annoyed. Even when attained, privacy was in itself suspicious. As Gowing writes, 'keys, locks, and bolts could furnish in themselves the causes of suspicion'.[22] This explains, in part, the tension the accomplices feel in scene 14 when the Mayor and the watchful community come knocking on the locked door: refusal to unlock the door and let the community in amplifies suspicion about domestic disorder.

Far from being a private sphere left to its own devices, the early modern home was understood as a political entity, analogous to the state. The properly governed household, according to contemporary moralists, was a 'school' where obedience and respect for social hierarchy were inculcated. The influential preacher and author of household guides William Gouge, for example, wrote that a family 'is as a school wherein the first principles and grounds of government and subjection are learned: whereby men are fitted to greater matters in Church or commonwealth'. In the domestic commonwealth, he added, the husband 'is as a king in his own house: as a king is to see that land well governed where he is king.'[23] In this context, infidelity within the home had public consequences, being a manifestation of the failure of domestic order. As an act of insubordination and rebellion against authority, it had the potential of setting an example of disobedience for servants, apprentices, children, and other dependants

[20] Laura Gowing, *Common Bodies: Women, Touch and Power in Seventeenth-Century England* (London: Yale University Press, 2013), 33.

[21] On Susan's double vulnerability, see Emma Whipday, 'Susan of Faversham: Staging Insubordination in *Arden*', in Kirwan and Salkeld (eds), *Arden of Faversham: A Critical Reader*, 111–12.

[22] Gowing, *Domestic Dangers*, 70–1.

[23] William Gouge, *Of Domesticall Duties* (London, 1622), sig. C1^{v}; S1^{v}.

within the home. As such, it threatened the hierarchies on which early modern order both inside and outside the home rested. When Mistress Arden rejects her wifely duty by providing poisonous meals, taking a lover, and finally killing her husband, it is not surprising that her servant Michael would first withdraw his deference and obedience to her then plan to poison her in a move which parallels her own rebellion. Following the murder and as Mistress Arden invites her dinner guests to sit to their meal, Michael turns to his fellow servant Susan, suggesting: 'let us sit down too' (14.285). Order within the household has collapsed, and this has implications for the social order at large. Nor was this analogy between house and state, husband and king, purely metaphorical. After 1352 and until 1790, 'petty treason' was the category under which murderous wives and servants were tried.[24] Male servants found guilty of petty treason were drawn to the place of execution on a hurdle, as a form of public shaming, then hanged. Wives and female servants were burned alive, the same punishment meted out to women who committed regicide, murder of the king. These are the punishments that the historical Mistress Arden and her servants suffered.[25]

Arden of Faversham explicitly engages with this conceptualization of the home as a political unit, the husband as king, and wives and servants as subjects. Both Master Arden and his murderers frame their motives and articulate their feelings in strikingly political language. Mistress Arden, for example, expresses exasperation with a husband who attempts to 'govern' her, opting, instead, to 'rule myself' (10.85). Later on, posing as a wronged wife, she describes herself to her husband as a 'Poor wench abused by thy misgovernment' (13.113). Master Arden understands Mosby's sojourn in his home as an act of political usurpation. Considering Franklin's advice to 'stay with me in London; go not home', Arden worries: 'Then that base Mosby doth usurp my room | And makes his triumph of my being thence' (4.28–30). His pun on 'room' fuses both the sense of his place as household head and his role as husband. The lovers demonstrate that this fear about usurpation of status and wife is well founded. Echoing Master Arden, Mosby suggests to Mistress Arden:

[24] On petty treason, see Frances E. Dolan, *Dangerous Familiars: Representations of Domestic Crime in England, 1550–1700* (Ithaca, NY: Cornell University Press, 1994), ch. 1.

[25] Wine (ed.), *Arden of Faversham*, 158.

'I hope, now Master Arden is from home, | You'll give me leave to play your husband's part.' She answers in kind: 'Mosby, you know who's master of my heart, | He well may be the master of the house' (1.631–4). This fantasy of sexual, social, and political replacement will be literalized following the murder when Mistress Arden places Mosby in her husband's chair: 'Master Mosby, sit you in my husband's seat' (14.282).

The overlapping nature of the public and the private is on display throughout the play. In the opening scene, the 'Love letters [which] passed 'twixt *Mosby* and my wife', as Master Arden confides in Franklin, are placed on a continuum with other documents, the 'letters patents from his majesty,' granting him 'All the lands of the Abbey of *Faversham*' (1.14, 5). Similarly, Master Arden's outrage and humiliation over the affair is not merely a result of the fact that his wife has taken a lover. It has a social dimension, for 'to dote on such a one as he | Is monstrous, *Franklin*, and intolerable'. As a 'botcher', that is a mender of clothing, and someone in 'service of a nobleman', Mosby's affair with Master Arden's wife is doubly insulting. The humiliation of being cuckolded by a social inferior seems to rankle more than the fact of wifely infidelity. Mosby himself will reveal his motives behind the affair and involvement in the murder to be more than the private matter of romantic love. In a soliloquy, he reveals his social ambitions by imagining his affair as akin to 'climb[ing] the top bough of the tree | And s[eeking] to build my nest among the clouds', an endeavour which, if unsuccessful, will result in his 'downfall to the earth' (8.15–16, 18). The social aspect to the sexual competition between Mosby and Master Arden is most visible when the latter confiscates the former's sword, citing legal prohibition against those below the rank of the gentry from carrying swords and instructing him, instead, to carry the tools associated with his humble trade, a needle and a pressing iron. It is instructive that in the murder scene, when the various murderers state the motives behind their involvement in the murder, Mosby does not name his love for Mistress Arden as she does. Instead, he harks back to this social insult: stabbing Master Arden, he informs him: 'There's for the pressing-iron you told me of' (14.231).

The public consequences of private desire are further highlighted through the playwrights' introduction, independent of their source, of a second love triangle involving Michael, Clarke, and Susan.

Similar to Master Arden and Mosby's competition, Clarke and Michael's is as much informed by sexual as by social rivalry. Echoing Master Arden, Clarke denigrates Michael as a 'serving-creature' (10.62), and Michael reproduces the sexual pun implicit in Mosby's 'sword' when he ridicules Clarke's phallic pencil as 'too weak' (72). Furthermore, Michael's desire for Susan not only motivates his involvement in the murderous plot on his master, but also forms the motive for another murder: killing his older brother in order to inherit his land. Michael's proposed murder of his father's heir is a crime against hierarchy and social order which resonates closely with master-murder.[26] Clarke, too, expresses eagerness to kill a social superior, Master Arden, in exchange for Susan's hand in marriage, providing the poison which is used for the first attempt on Master Arden's life as well as a poisoned crucifix which is never used. The intertwining of the social and the sexual is stressed again when Black Will fantasizes about how 'sweet Alice Arden, with a lap of crowns, | Comes with a lowly curtsy to the earth | Saying, "Take this but for thy quarterage"' (3.88–90). In the world of *Arden*, private desire is indistinguishable from its social context and the personal is also political.[27]

'That plot of ground which thou detains from me': Tenants and Landlords

The connection between Master Arden's domestic rule and his public role as landlord is registered in the nature of his government both inside and outside his home as well as in the fact that both members of his household and members of the community join forces to murder him. Holinshed insisted on calling the murder 'but a private matter', and later retellings, including the play's title-page, attempted to pin the murder on Alice Arden (the 'disloyal and wanton wife'), thus 'purging' it of its non-domestic elements.[28] Arden's murder, however, is brought about by his failure of government both within his home

[26] Frank Whigham, *Seizures of the Will in Early Modern English Drama* (Cambridge: Cambridge University Press, 1996), 89.

[27] Michael Neill, '"This Gentle Gentleman": Social Change and the Language of Status in *Arden of Faversham*,' *Medieval and Renaissance Drama in England*, 10 (1998), 90–1.

[28] Orlin, *Private Matters and Public Culture*, 64.

and outside it. The play establishes Master Arden's ineffectiveness as a domestic king by repeatedly showing him 'tak[ing] horse' and departing the site of disorder that is his home, instead of dealing with its cause: the presence of Mosby, his wife's lover, in the home (1.49).[29] Furthermore, despite identifying Susan, the Ardens' maidservant and Mosby's sister, as a disruptive presence in his home and vowing: 'Come I once at home, | I'll rouse her from remaining in my house', he never does that (3.29–30). Additionally, Master Arden repeatedly allows himself to be manipulated by his wife into reconciling with Mosby and permitting his visits to continue, even urging him to 'frequent it [his house] more' so as 'The world shall see that I distrust her [Alice] not' (1.347–8). Even when given the perverse advice to abandon his home and accompany Franklin to London and recognizing it as 'abhor[ring] from reason', Master Arden acts on it, leaving Mosby to enjoy his home and wife (1.53).[30] While the play's source, Holinshed's *Chronicles*, states that Master Arden deliberately 'winke[d] at her [Alice's] filthy disorder, and both permitted and also invited Mosby very often to lodge in his house' because of the 'benefit' he gained 'at some of her friends' [i.e. family's] hands', there is no such explanation for his behaviour in the play (Wine, ed., 149). This seeming lack of logic to his ineffectiveness has baffled critics, so much so that it has been suggested that Master Arden only feigns outrage at the affair and that, in reality, he allows it to continue in hopes it will produce an heir, something he himself is unable to accomplish. The play certainly omits any mention of the two daughters the historical Arden had, leaving him heirless, and Mistress Arden's reference to the children who, she fantasizes, her husband's 'bags of gold' will 'make . . . rich' has been interpreted as referring to her future children with Mosby, not any existing ones with Arden. Be that as it may, Master Arden proves an inefficient king in his home, and this is reflected in his inefficiency outside it as well.

[29] Ann C. Christensen reads those repeated departures as forming the context for domestic disorder. See *Separation Scenes: Domestic Drama in Early Modern England* (Lincoln, Neb. and London: University of Nebraska Press, 2017).

[30] Some critics have argued that Arden is partially culpable for his demise based on such inaction on his part. See Julie R. Schutzman, 'Alice Arden's Freedom and the Suspended Moment of *Arden of Faversham*', *Studies in English Literature, 1500–1900*, 36/2 (1996), 304; Orlin, *Private Matters and Public Culture*, 97.

The play opens with the conferral of the Faversham Abbey lands on Master Arden: 'My gracious Lord, the Duke of *Somerset,* | Hath freely given to thee and to thy heirs, | By letters patents from his majesty, | All the lands of the Abbey of *Faversham*' (1.2–5). This event confirms Master Arden's status as one of the 'new men' who came to social prominence and financial prosperity following Henry VIII's dissolution of the monasteries and sale of monastic land in the 1530s. The play's engagement with this important historical moment renders it a history play dealing directly with the consequences of the dissolution of the monasteries and its sudden transformation of land from a sign of the aristocracy into a commodity.[31] The historical Arden was a public figure. He served under Sir Edward North in the Court of Augmentations, managing the revenue and litigation relating to the dissolution of monastic lands, and was appointed to the position of controller of the customs for Faversham port (where he spends some time in the play unloading goods (1.88–9, 220–1)), and mayor of Faversham in 1548. The play shows Master Arden's possession of the lands as resulting in the dispossession of previous tenants, Master Greene and Dick Reede. It is from these two characters that our view of him as a public man, landlord, and neighbour emerges. Master Greene, whose land has recently been granted to Arden, describes him to his wife as 'greedy-gaping still for gain; | Nor cares he, though young gentlemen do beg, | So he may scrape and hoard up in his pouch'; 'Desire of wealth is endless in his mind' (1.472–5). This assessment is confirmed in scene 13 when Dick Reede, another dispossessed tenant, intercepts Master Arden outside his home ('He never will vouchsafe to speak with me' otherwise), begging him to let him have 'the plot of ground | Which wrongfully you detain from me', for 'Although the rent of it be very small, | Yet will it help my wife and childëren, | Which here I leave in Faversham, God knows, | Needy and bare' (13.6, 12–17). Master Arden's cruelty and abdication of his social responsibility are captured in his harsh response: he first dismisses the man's grievances as mere 'rail[ing]', then threatens to 'lay thee up so close a twelvemonth's day | As thou shalt neither see the sun nor moon', further promising: 'Look to it, for, as surely as I live, | I'll banish pity if thou use me thus' (13.24–7). As such, Master Arden is shown mismanaging his public role and abandoning

[31] See Whigham, *Seizures of the Will*, 63, 77.

his duties as a landlord. In a similar way to the home, where the head of the household acts as a benign 'father' to his 'family', the maintenance of social order rested on the landlord's performance of his duties towards his tenants.[32] Polly Findlay's 2014 RSC production replaced Reede with his wife Mrs Reede. Where the textual Arden insults Reede as a 'knave', Ian Redford's Arden called Lizzie Hopley's Mrs Reede a 'witch', highlighting Arden's dangerous misogyny in addition to his cruelty. The play confirms both Greene and Reede's assessment of Master Arden's greed and selfishness as well as validating their claims when it frames the murder as fulfilment of Reede's curse that 'That plot of ground which thou detains from me… | Be ruinous and fatal unto thee! | Either there be butchered by thy dearest friends, | Or else be brought for men to wonder at' (13.32–6). The Epilogue informs the audience that 'Arden lay murdered in that plot of ground | Which he by force and violence held from Reede', thus discrediting Arden's claim that he 'ne'er did him wrong' and problematizing the title's moralistic message about the murder being the work of a 'wanton wife' by framing it as divine punishment for his greed and lack of charity (13.57). In this version, Alice becomes an instrument of divine retribution.

'narrow-prying neighbour blabs': Household and Neighbourhood

Arden stages the relationship between the disordered home and its neighbourhood as one of tension and mutual suspicion. In the opening exchange between Master Arden and Franklin, in which his social rise in the world is solidified by royal grant of the abbey lands, Master Arden confides in his friend his grief over the fact that the community is taking interest in the disorder within his home and that the affair causes him to be 'pointed at' (1.34). Later, he frets over 'all the knights and gentlemen of Kent [who] | Make common table-talk of' the affair (1.341–2). Similarly, Mistress Arden, when she momentarily seems to regret her affair with Mosby and decide to turn into 'honest Arden's wife', also evokes the ill name the affair has earned her in the community, reprimanding Mosby for 'ma[king] me slanderous to all my kin' (8.72, 74). The suspicion between the home and the

[32] See Garrett A. Sullivan, '*Arden of Faversham* and the Early Modern Household', in Garrett A. Sullivan, Patrick Cheney, and Andrew Hadfield (eds), *Early Modern English Drama: A Critical Companion* (Oxford: Oxford University Press, 2005), 77.

neighbourhood is mutual. Mistress Arden is keenly aware of her 'narrow-prying neighbour[s]', those whose spatial proximity to her house makes them witnesses and observers of her transgressions. Following their reconciliation in scene 8, Mistress Arden suggests: 'Come, let us in to shun suspicïon', attempting to hide her affair from her neighbours' watchful eyes (164). The irony is that seeking privacy, shutting windows, and locking doors intensified neighbourly suspicion instead of preventing it. The ultimate irony is that the offstage audience are positioned as the watchful, observant community who, even as Mistress Arden shuts her doors against her onstage neighbours, follow her and Mosby into the space imagined onstage as 'inside'. Thus the very nature of the theatre works to undermine a disordered household's attempt to guard its secrets and conceal them from the community.

Arden's characters, regardless of social standing, are obsessed with their 'credit' or 'reputation'. In a society where most commercial transactions were oral and informal, credit, a term which fuses the moral and the financial, was crucial.[33] Master Arden worries about the 'common speech of men | (Who mangle credit with their wounding words | And couch dishonour as dishonour buds)' (4.4–5). Mosby, too, regrets the loss of his reputation resulting from his affair with Mistress Arden: 'Let me repent the credit I have lost' (8.81). The play contrasts Mistress Arden's disregard for oaths and vows ('oaths are words, and words is wind, | And wind is mutable. Then I conclude | 'Tis childishness to stand upon an oath' (1.434–6)), itself a threat to the social order, with other characters' dogged commitment to their (wicked) promises. Even the hired assassins, Black Will and Shakebag, subscribe to a parodic version of this obsession with credit. Following the apprentice's lowering of his shop window on Black Will's head which results in a bloody forehead, Black Will regrets accepting ten pounds as a fee for the murder: 'I value every drop of my blood at a French crown. I have had ten pound to steal a dog, and we have no more here to kill a man.' However, he decides, 'a bargain is a bargain', and he cannot renege on his word (3.69–70). Similarly, Michael decides to put aside his conscience pangs over granting the assassins access to his master in the night, for

[33] Craig Muldrew, *The Economy of Obligation: The Culture of Credit and Social Relations in Early Modern England* (London: Macmillan Press, 1998), 96.

'So have I sworn to Mosby and my mistress; | So have I promised to the slaughtermen' (3.196–7).

Following the murder in scene 14, *Arden* stages the community invading the disordered home and defeating the murderers' attempts to conceal incriminating evidence. Importantly, this is staged against an attempt by Mistress Arden to maintain a fantasy of cooperative, neighbourly relationships. Before he arrives home to what turns out to be his murder, Master Arden has offered Mosby a reconciliatory dinner to which he has also invited several neighbours, an exercise in hospitality which affirms his role in the community and cements his social ties. Following the murder, Mistress Arden strives to maintain a façade of hospitable domesticity which affords her the authority to stage manage her interactions with her neighbours and control her space. She takes control of the seating plan: 'Master Bradshaw, sit you there. | I pray you be content, I'll have my will. | Master Mosby, sit you in my husband's seat' (180–2). However, the façade quickly shatters when the Mayor and members of the community arrive to search the house. Significantly, the Mayor's stated purpose is to search for Black Will, a masterless figure whose vagrant status marked him as a criminal in early modern law.[34] He stands not only outside the home, but also in opposition to it: both Black Will and Shakebag are constructed as a danger to familial bonds, for they offer: 'if thou'lt have thy own father slain that thou mayest inherit his land, we'll kill him'; 'Ay, thy mother, thy sister, thy brother, or all thy kin' (2.85–7). The presence of Black Will in the Ardens' home alerts the watchful community to the disorder within even before they become aware of the murder. The play stages Mistress Arden's misjudged relief that it is only Black Will, not her husband's corpse, they search for ('I am glad it is no worse' (14.364)). However, the fact that the Ardens' home welcomes the likes of Black Will sends a signal to the community that this house is misgoverned, and intervention is required.

In *Arden*, as in other domestic tragedies, it is the community that is staged as first getting suspicious that something is not right within the individual household, identifying the transgression (often murder), collecting forensic evidence, interpreting clues, and apprehending the murderers. This was an example of the early modern playhouse

[34] On vagrancy in early modern England, see A. L. Beier, *Masterless Men: The Vagrancy Problem in England 1560–1640* (London and New York: Methuen, 1985).

making an intervention into contemporary debates surrounding lay participation in the judiciary system. In the late sixteenth and early seventeenth centuries, playwrights offered playgoers stories which position lay people, rather than professional magistrates, as effective administrators of justice. The early modern playhouse was a space particularly suited to exploring concepts of communal justice, thanks to the embodied nature of playgoing, of witnessing, feeling, listening with others in the same space, and the way plays often situate their audiences as judges of the action they witness on stage.[35] For example, *Arden*'s Epilogue explicitly singles out to the audience certain aspects of the story which 'above the rest [are] to be noted' as they are invited to pass their own judgement on what they saw (9). In Holinshed's *Chronicles*, it is the Mayor who performs the various elements of evidence collection and interpretation which we associate with criminal investigation. For example, Holinshed reports that it is the Mayor who 'commanded every man to stay' while 'appoint[ing] some to go about, and to come in at the side of the house through the garden…where Master Arden's dead body did lie', leading to the discovery of the incriminating footprints in the snow. It is the Mayor also who 'with others went to the flower de lice, where they found Mosby in bed [with] his hose and purse stained with some of Master Aarden's blood'.[36] *Arden*'s playwrights, however, position the community, rather than the Mayor, as performing this role. It is Franklin who concludes Master Arden must have been 'murdered in this house | And carried to the fields, for from that place | Backwards and forwards may you see | The print of many feet within the snow' (14.389–92). Moreover, he urges the gathered community to 'look about this chamber where we are, | And you shall find part of his guiltless blood', an invitation to which the Mayor responds, announcing: 'Look in the place where he was wont to sit. | See, see! His blood! It is too manifest' (393–4, 397–8). Franklin reveals further clues he has been able to collect: 'in his slip-shoe did I find some rushes, | Which argueth he was murdered in this room' (395–6). The Mayor becomes a recipient of reports provided by the community, acting on the information they supply. Similarly, in the domestic plot of Robert

[35] Penelope Geng, *Communal Justice in Shakespeare's England: Drama, Law, and Emotion* (Toronto: University of Toronto Press, 2021), xii–xi, 92.

[36] In Wine (ed.), *The Tragedy of Arden of Faversham*, 157–8.

Yarrington's *Two Lamentable Tragedies* (*c.*1594), it is the victim's neighbours who lead the investigation into his murder, gathering evidence, interpreting clues, and knocking on doors in search of suspects, eventually identifying the murderer and his accomplice.[37] Given the early modern investment in the notion of the 'moral community' and the ideal of neighbourly watchfulness, it is not surprising that domestic tragedies often stage the community itself rooting out disorder, identifying transgressors, and demonstrating agency in their arrest and eventual punishment.

'it was cunningly performed': Alice Arden

At the heart of accounts of Master Arden's murder lies his wife, Mistress Arden. *Arden* is no exception. Her role is the longest in the play, and one of the longest early modern roles for a female character.[38] The play's moralizing title-page singles her out for blame, describing her as a 'disloyal and wanton', 'wicked' wife whose 'great malice and dissimulation', 'unsatiable desire', and 'filthy lust' lead to her 'shameful end'. The moral judgement attaching to Mistress Arden is a legacy of the play's source, where Holinshed, in marginal comments in the text, describes her as an 'Importunate & bloody minded strumpet!', urging the reader to 'Mark what a countenance of innocence and ignorance she bore after the murdering of her husband' in order to 'colour her wickedness'.[39] It is important to pay attention to the way Mistress Arden's challenge to her wifely role and her husband's authority are constructed in the play. Mistress Arden conceives of her rebellion as a bid for freedom from the cage that is marriage. In this rhetoric, the affair with Mosby becomes a legitimate bond, while marriage to Master Arden becomes a violation of that bond: 'Sweet Mosby is the man that hath my heart, | And [Arden] he usurps it, having nought but this: | That I am tied to him by marrïage' (1.97–9). In a classic essay, Catherine Belsey has argued that Alice Arden's murder of her husband attracted attention not because of the details of the murder or the degree of premeditation involved.

[37] Robert Yarrington, *Two Lamentable Tragedies*, ed. Chiaki Hanabusa (Manchester: Manchester University Press for the Malone Society, 2013), sig. G3^v.

[38] See this edition, p. 39.

[39] In Wine (ed.), *The Tragedy of Arden of Faversham*, 154, 156.

Instead, she asserted, 'the scandal lies in Alice Arden's challenge to the institution of marriage' and 'her flagrant defiance of the marriage bond' at a time when divorce as we know it today, allowing remarriage, did not exist.[40] At first, Mistress Arden's goal appears to be autonomy and self-determination: 'Why should' Arden, she wonders, 'govern me that am to rule myself?' (10.83, 85). However, as the play progresses and the various murderers' motives become clear, Mistress Arden seems to simply prefer Mosby's 'title' to Arden's: 'Love is a god, and marriage is but words; | And therefore *Mosby's* title is the best' (1.100–1). Her use of 'title' suggests that she has internalized patriarchy's construction of women as possessions and coincides with Master Arden's own designation of land and wife as one category of possession and means of validation of his masculinity and social status implicit in his redirecting the conversation about lands initiated by Mosby into one about wives ('As for the lands, Mosby, they are mine | By letters patents from his majesty. | But I must have a mandate [an official order signifying ownership] for my wife' (1.298–300)).[41]

Throughout the play, Mistress Arden emerges as a self-conscious performer. As Terri Bourus writes, 'Alice is fascinating because of her intensity and volatility, and the difficulty of distinguishing between her various performances: we never know, and she may not either, who is the "real" Alice.'[42] She skilfully manipulates and uses existing cultural scripts surrounding women and domesticity to her advantage. One of those cultural scripts is directly connected with narratives of petty treason, that of the battered, wronged wife, badly treated by her tyrannical husband. In pamphlet accounts of husband-murder cases, murderous wives, while repenting their murderous transgressions, often voice the misery and desperation of their married lives which, they maintain, led to them finally murdering their abusive husbands. Narratives of petty tyrants were the counterpart of those of petty traitors.[43] While petty tyranny ending in wife murder was not

[40] Catherine Belsey, *The Subject of Tragedy: Identity and Difference in Renaissance Drama* (London: Methuen, 1985), 130–1.

[41] Peter Stallybrass, 'Patriarchal Territories: The Body Enclosed', in Margaret Ferguson, Maureen Quilligan, and Nancy Vickers (eds), *Rewriting the Renaissance: The Discourse of Sexual Difference in Early Modern Europe* (Chicago: University of Chicago Press), 123–42.

[42] Terri Bourus, '*Arden of Faversham* by Royal Shakespeare Company (review)', *Shakespeare Bulletin*, 33/4 (2015), 695.

[43] Dolan, *Dangerous Familiars*, ch. 3.

distinguished in law as a separate category of crime the way petty treason was, it carried cultural weight and often mobilized neighbours to come to the help of battered wives.[44] On more than one occasion, Mistress Arden adopts the role of the battered wife, momentarily changing the plot of the play she is in into one about wife murder, similar to that staged in another domestic tragedy, Thomas Middleton's *A Yorkshire Tragedy* (1605). In the opening scene, she adopts this role when confronting her husband following his detection of the poison in the breakfast broth she has offered him: 'There's nothing that I do can please your taste. | You were best to say I would have poisoned you', before she switches to the third person singular, complaining about her alleged mistreatment to the onstage and, by extension, the offstage audience: 'I cannot speak or cast aside my eye, | But he imagines I have stepped awry' (1.366–9). She even expresses a suicidal wish, offering to 'eat of it [the broth] myself' and wishing: 'Would it were full of poison to the brim! | Then should my cares and troubles have an end', before she asks rhetorically: 'Was ever silly woman so tormented?' (1.384–7). Later on, she will put on the same performance for the benefit of her neighbour Master Greene: 'Ah, Master Greene—be it spoken in secret here— | I never live good day with him alone.' He is, she reveals, verbally and physically abusive: 'When he is at home, then have I froward looks, | Hard words, and blows.' Moreover, she alleges that he is unfaithful, 'keep[ing] in every corner trulls', 'filthy ones' who 'counsels him to make away his wife', thus causing her to 'live... daily in continual fear, | In sorrow' and pushing her to the extremes of despair: 'As every day I wish with hearty prayer | That he or I were taken forth the world' (1.490–503). In manipulating existing cultural narratives and using them to her advantage, Mistress Arden succeeds in recruiting the already embittered Master Greene into her murderous plans, casting him in the role of knight-in-shining-armour and herself as a helpless damsel-in-distress, a role he embraces enthusiastically: 'frolic, woman, I shall be the man | Shall set you free from all this discontent' (509–10).

Mistress Arden is also constructed as an anti-wife and an anti-household mistress. The obverse of the ideal wife who was understood as obedient to her husband and an efficient manager of her household, Mistress Arden performs her duties in a way which perverts the

[44] See Gowing, *Domestic Dangers*, 215.

very nature of housewifery. For example, she serves her husband breakfast, only to poison him. Instead of carefully supervising domestic goods and preserving the fruit of her husband's hard work as the good wife was supposed to do, she only mentions her husband's labour within the context of planning the descent of its profit to her future children with Mosby ('My saving husband hoards up bags of gold | To make our children rich', she reassures Mosby (1.219–20)). Emblematizing this perversion of her wifely duty, she conceals the assassins in her husband's counting house before the murder is carried out, thus granting them access to one of the most private and exclusive spaces within the home and laying her husband's wealth open to them. Mistress Arden's undermining of housewifery culminates in her kneeling on the bloodstained floor following the murder as she performs, together with her maidservant, Susan, a perverted, twisted version of a domestic chore, attempting unsuccessfully to remove evidence of the crime (14.252). This aspect was stressed in Polly Findlay's 2014 production for the RSC in which Susan's routine tasks, dusting furniture items, cleaning, and mopping turn into tasks aimed at concealing murder.

Throughout the play, Mistress Arden is cast in the role of antimistress. She is the embodiment at every turn of all that a household mistress and employer of domestic servants should not be. The institution of service existed in early modern England partly to contain and discipline the harmful and disruptive urges and inclinations associated with youth. The perception of service as morally beneficial was closely connected with the perception of the household as a spiritual as well as an emotional and economic institution. Its master and mistress were charged with the moral and religious education of their servants (as well as children). Mistress Arden embodies the antithesis of this ideal when she tears up her prayer book. In the Ardens' household, the mistress does not use her prayer book to perform collective devotional exercises with her servants. Instead, she destroys it and with it her spiritual role in relation to them. Moreover, instead of being herself an example of moral uprightness and an active agent in shaping her servants' spiritual lives, Mistress Arden is cast in the role of negative exemplar. She is engaged in the spiritually damning act of turning them into murderers. Intent on murdering her husband, Mistress Arden converts her servants into fellow assassins, bribing Michael with Susan's hand in marriage

('On that condition, Michael, here is my hand: | None shall have Mosby's sister but thyself (1.146–7)) and involving Susan after the fact by enlisting her help in cleaning the murder scene and removing the body to the fields.

Mistress Arden is also cast in the role of the anti-type to the responsible household mistress described in conduct literature. While servants were expected to be single (those who married, and especially those who became pregnant, facing dismissal in most cases), it was generally accepted that it was part of the good master's and mistress's duties towards their servants to help them to a good marriage.[45] Most servants had come to the city of London to get a position in service. Distance from the parental home, combined with the real possibility that their parents may have died before or during their period in service, meant that, for many servants, masters and mistresses acted as proxy parents.[46] Mistress Arden perverts this duty when she promises her maidservant Susan to two suitors at the same time. Not concerned in the least about Susan's welfare or happiness in either match, she offers her simply as a pawn to bind both her servant Michael and the painter and maker of poisons, Clarke. The 2014 RSC emphasized Mistress Arden's (Sharon Small) complete lack of sensitivity to her maidservant's desires by staging a Susan who was utterly terrified by Clarke (Christopher Middleton) and clearly in love with Michael (Ian Bonar). On stage for most of the performance, engaged in domestic chores, Susan bangs her head against the table she crouches under to mop the floor when she overhears Clarke asking her mistress for her hand in marriage. By contrast, she and Michael take every opportunity they can to touch each other and kiss, including when Master Arden (Ian Redford) sits down to his last supper.

'Thou art not fair: I viewed thee not till now': *Racialized Transgressions*

While *Arden* is not explicitly a play about race, it appeared on the English stage at a time when England was experiencing increased contact with the world through trade, piracy, and early experiments in

[45] Keith Wrightson, *English Society, 1580–1680* (London and New York: Routledge, 2003), 94.

[46] See Gowing, *Domestic Dangers*, 15.

slavery as part of what has been termed an 'emergent globalization'.[47] Dramatized encounters between white, Christian Europeans and racialized others were increasingly on offer on the English stage at the end of the sixteenth and the early seventeenth centuries. This is evidenced by the phenomenon of Turk plays (plays concerned with interactions between Muslims and Christians set in Ottoman lands and addressing questions of conversion and piracy as well as interracial desire). Shakespeare's *Othello*, staging a Black hero engaged in a European struggle against the Ottoman enemy imagined at the beginning of the play as threatening Cyprus, testifies to an appetite for such stories.[48] This increased interest should not be surprising as peoples of non-European descent were not only encountered on global shores, but were also a visible presence in early modern England. The pioneering work of historian Imtiaz Habib has revealed that Black people were 'a pervasive, repetitive, and accelerating presence in Elizabethan London'.[49] 'Black Tudors'—Africans in Tudor England—as later scholars building on Habib's work have shown, 'were not only present, but played an active part in some of the best-known stories of the age.'[50] Such relatively well-known Africans include John Blanke, the trumpeter depicted in the Westminster Tournament Roll of 1511; Thomasen, a Black maid in Elizabeth I's court (1574–7); and the Moroccan ambassador to Elizabeth I, Abd el-Ouahed ben Messaoud ben Mohammed Anoun, often credited with being Shakespeare's inspiration for Othello.[51] The Black presence in the period was not restricted to those few who made it to such prestigious positions. African men and women often performed functional roles as porters, gardeners, musicians, cooks, or laundresses. We can glimpse them in such characters as the Prince of Morocco in Shakespeare's *The Merchant of Venice* as well as Desdemona's childhood maidservant Barbary in *Othello* and Caliban's mother Sycorax in *The Tempest*.

[47] Emily C. Bartels, *Speaking of the Moor: From Alcazar to Othello* (Philadelphia: University of Pennsylvania Press, 2008), 17.

[48] On Turk plays, see Matthew Dimmock, *New Turkes: Dramatizing Islam and the Ottomans in Early Modern England* (Aldershot: Ashgate, 2005).

[49] Imtiaz Habib, *Black Lives in the English Archives, 1500–1677: Imprints of the Invisible* (Aldershot: Routledge, 2008), 116.

[50] Miranda Kaufmann, *Black Tudors: The Untold Story* (London: OneWorld Publications, 2017), 262.

[51] E. A. J. Honigmann, 'Introduction' to *Othello*, Arden Third Series (London: Methuen, 1997), 1–112; 2–4, 14–17; Habib, *Black Lives*, 2.

Although no somatically marked character appears in *Arden*, the play participates in early modern processes of race-making, registering its culture's anxieties about racial otherness by employing racial epithets to frame the lovers' quarrel in scene 8.

In his account of the murder, Holinshed, as literary critic Brandi K. Adams has observed, 'shapes a narrative about English whiteness and fairness, fidelity in marriage and fears about racialized others which disrupt both the English domestic sphere and the state at large'. While he describes the Ardens as 'an embodiment of English perfection', Holinshed refers to Mosby as 'black swart man', thus 'marking him both as a racialized other and as evil, since "swart" also connoted "ill will" '.[52] This description is abandoned in the play as no such reference to a somatically marked Mosby appears. Socially and sexually transgressive characters, however, are racialized in ways which elide the threat they pose to ordered marriages, homes, and communities with the perceived threat posed to England by Black individuals. This treatment applies to both Mosby and Mistress Arden.

Early in the play, Mosby is positioned as 'other' through association with England's racialized and demonized enemy, Spain. Reprimanding Mosby for presumptuously carrying a sword, a privilege reserved in early modern England for the ranks of the gentry and above ('So, sirrah, you may not wear a sword! | The statute makes against artificers' (1.308–9)), Master Arden confiscates the weapon, suggesting, instead, that, as tailor, Mosby should, among other tools, use his 'Spanish needle' (311). Master Arden's instruction that a needle is more appropriate for Mosby to brandish than a sword is clearly sexually suggestive, casting doubt on his sexual potency as well as associating him with women and housewifery. It is also racially charged given that the needle is specifically described as 'Spanish'. In the late sixteenth century Hispanophobia was rife, and early modern drama played an important role in disseminating anti-Spanish sentiment, most famously in Thomas Kyd's *The Spanish Tragedy*.[53] Spain was associated with racial impurity and religious otherness. The anti-Spanish

[52] Brandi K. Adams, '"What manner of man was he?": Will and the Making of Archival Blackness in *Arden of Faversham*', in Kirwan and Duncan (eds), *Arden of Faversham: A Critical Reader*, 145.

[53] Eric J. Griffin, *English Renaissance Drama and the Specter of Spain: Ethnopoetics and Empire* (Philadelphia: University of Pennsylvania Press, 2009), 1.

discourse known as the Black Legend of Spanish Cruelty asserted that 'Spaniards were unusually cruel, avaricious, treacherous, fanatical, superstitious, cowardly, corrupt, decadent, indolent, and authoritarian.'[54] The play insistently associates Mosby with those qualities. His adultery with Mistress Arden raises the spectre of a contaminated bloodline, and his intrusion into Mistress Arden's marriage, she claims, ruins her previously loving marital union with Arden: 'The heavens can witness, and the world can tell, | Before I saw that falsehood look of thine, | 'Fore I was tangled with thy 'ticing speech, | Arden to me was dearer than my soul, | And shall be still' (1.193–7). His tyrannical, bloodthirsty character is revealed in his plans to eliminate those who have helped him to Master Arden's 'seat' once he has achieved it: 'I can cast a bone | To make these curs [Michael and Clarke] pluck out each other's throat; | And then am I sole ruler of mine own', lest they should 'insult upon me for my meed | Or fright me by detecting of his end' (8.32–6). More disturbingly, he also plans to 'cleanly rid my hands of her [Alice]', for she has 'supplanted Arden for my sake | And will extirpen me to plant another' (8.43, 40–1). Mosby's Spanish needle also links him with England's racial and religious others, the Moors. In the early modern imagination, Spain's historical association with the Islamic world of the Moors tainted it with Blackness, rendering it the opposite of white England. Thus in Edmund Spenser's *A View of the State of Ireland* (1596), the Spanish are described as 'the most mingled, most uncertain, most bastardlie' nation under heaven, one marked indelibly by its Moorish invaders.[55] Readers will recall Shakespeare's Othello, who is also a Moor and whose history of the fated handkerchief, like Mosby's needle, links him with practices of spinning and weaving.[56] For playgoers familiar with Turk plays framing Moors as a danger to white, English identity, Mosby would have sounded like a domestic version of the same threat, poised on undermining the white, English home.

'Fair' is often used in the play to suggest beauty and sexual desirability. Thus when Master Greene first learns about the abuse

[54] David J. Weber, *The Spanish Frontier in North America* (New Haven: Yale University Press, 1992), 336.

[55] Edmund Spenser, *A View of the State of Ireland*, ed. Andrew Hadfield and Willy Maley (Oxford: Blackwell, 1997), 50.

[56] William Shakespeare, *Othello*, ed. Gary Taylor, in *The New Oxford Shakespeare*, 3.4.50–68.

Mistress Arden allegedly experiences at her husband's hands, his outrage seems to centre on the way her 'fairness' is so slighted: 'Now trust me, Mistress Alice, it grieveth me | So fair a creature should be so abused' (1.504–5). Similarly, Susan's 'fairness' is singled out by Clarke as constituting a major part of her appeal as a partner (and incentive to crime): 'if fair Susan and I can make a gree, | You shall command me to the uttermost | As far as either goods or life may stretch' (1.545–7). The positive qualities associated with 'fairness' are suggested through such phrases as 'Entreat her fair', 'fair words', 'fair weather', and 'fair means' (1.45, 541; 10.44; 13.64). Kim F. Hall, in her field-defining book *Things of Darkness: Economies of Race and Gender in Early Modern England*, has taught us to read the binary of 'foul' and 'fair' in early modern texts as a 'site of crucial delineations of cultural difference', describing the 'binarism of black and white' as 'the originary language of racial difference in English culture'.[57] Those binaries are often at work in early modern drama where white women's unruly sexuality renders them unworthy of whiteness and the privileges which accompany it, such as sexual desirability, and inscribes them within a discourse of inferior Blackness, the pre-modern code for everything negative.[58] In Shakespeare's *Titus Andronicus*, for example, Tamora's, the Queen of the Goths and later the Roman Empress, transgressive sexuality emblematized in her affair with Aaron, a Moorish slave, taints her whiteness, transforming her into a version of her Black lover.[59] Outlining the way her liaison with Aaron taints her whiteness, Bassianus taunts her: 'Believe me, queen, your swarth Cimmerian | Doth make your honour of his body's hue, | Spotted, detested and abominable' (2.3.72–4). The early modern stage used various techniques to imitate Black skin, such as black cloth which covered the player's white body and skin-blackening agents, such as 'charred cork mixed with a little oil'.[60] It would not be too far-fetched to imagine the latter staining the white

[57] Kim F. Hall, *Things of Darkness: Economies of Race and Gender in Early Modern England* (Ithaca, NY: Cornell University Press, 1995), 177, 2, 6.

[58] On whiteness as a property which provides material benefits, see Cheryl I. Harris, 'Whiteness as Property', *Harvard Law Review*, 106/8 (1993), 1709–91.

[59] Ian Smith, 'Othello's Black Handkerchief', *Shakespeare Quarterly*, 64/1 (2013), 1–25.

[60] Dympna Callaghan, *Shakespeare without Women: Representing Gender and Race on the Renaissance Stage* (New York: Routledge, 2000), 78.

skin of the players who interacted with the 'Black' character. As such, Aaron's 'tainting' of Tamora's white body might actually have been literal.

In *Arden*, Mistress Arden's transgression similarly taints her whiteness. While Master Arden restricts his insults to the sexual ('Injurious strumpet', he rails at her (13.78)), it is Mosby who uses racial epithets to express his anger at her. For him, Mistress Arden's transgressive sexuality does not taint her whiteness as long as it benefits him, both sexually and socially. However, when she enters the stage in scene 8 carrying her prayer book, an emblem of spousal virtue, and informs him that she intends to return to her 'former happy life again, | From title of an odious strumpet's name | To "honest Arden's wife"', Mosby immediately resorts to racialized insults, employing the racially charged binary of fair/foul (8.70–3).[61] 'Thou art not fair', he informs her, 'I viewed thee not till now'; 'It grieves me not to see how foul thou art, | But mads me that I ever thought thee fair' (8.97, 101–2). The 'dove' which Mosby thought his lover to be, he realizes, is really a 'raven' (96). In Mosby's case, what alienates Mistress Arden from whiteness and the privileges it affords, including the right to sexual fulfilment and desirability, is not disloyalty or betrayal. It is repentance and conversion into the feminine ideal of marital chastity which bring about this racial turning. Ironically, in early modern accounts of conversion, repentance instead *confers* whiteness on the convert. In *Steps to the Temple* (1646), Richard Crashaw describes the conversion of an African man as whitening his soul:

> Let it no longer be a forlorn hope
> To wash an Ethiope:
> He's washt, His gloomy skin a peaceful shade
> For his white soul is made:
> And now, I doubt not, the Eternal Dove,
> A black-fac'd house will love.[62]

Conversion, then, produces a living contradiction, a person who is externally black and internally white.[63] In his inverted theology,

[61] Elizabeth Williamson, 'The Uses and Abuses of Prayer Book Properties in *Hamlet*, *Richard III*, and *Arden of Faversham*', *English Literary Renaissance*, 39/2 (2009), 391.

[62] Richard Crashaw, *Steps to the Temple* (London, 1646), sig. B4^v.

[63] Ania Loomba, *Shakespeare, Race, and Colonialism* (Oxford: Oxford University Press, 2002), 56.

Mosby demonstrates his deviation from the religious values of the Reformation even as he reinforces the early modern association between wilful women and racial otherness. By inserting both Mosby and Mistress Arden within discourses of racialized otherness, *Arden* performs the cultural work, also familiar from such plays as *Othello*, of distancing whiteness and Englishness from illicit and murderous sexuality, unruly femininity, and, in the case of Othello, murderous jealousy and irrationality.

'you served me well': Servants

The early modern family, like the Ardens', often included household servants. They were members of their master's 'family', a term which contemporaries used to describe the entire household, rather than to refer only to relatives by blood or marriage in the modern sense.[64] Household service, according to historians' estimates, was undertaken by no less than 60 per cent of the population aged 15 to 24. They were to be found in 29 per cent of all households in the period.[65] The institution of service occupied a central position in early modern English society. This was a society, according to historian Kevin Sharpe, 'organized around service relationships'.[66] This fact was best expressed by a contemporary moralist who stated: 'even they who are superiors to some, are inferiors to others'.[67] Household servants occupied positions which ranged widely in terms of status and pay from the humblest kitchen maid and maid-of-all-work as the Ardens' Susan seems to be to the officials of the aristocratic households pulled from the ranks of the gentry and nobility, the stewards such as Shakespeare's Malvolio in *Twelfth Night* and Mosby, who, according to the bitter, thus not wholly trustworthy, Master Arden, 'Crept into service of a nobleman, | And by his servile flattery and fawning |

[64] Keith Wrightson, *Earthly Necessities: Economic Lives in Early Modern Britain* (New Haven: Yale University Press, 2000), 33.

[65] See Ann Kussmaul, *Servants in Husbandry in Early Modern England* (Cambridge: Cambridge University Press, 1981), 3; Peter Laslett, *The World We Have Lost: Further Explored* (London: Taylor & Francis, 2001), 13–16.

[66] Kevin Sharpe, *Remapping Early Modern England: The Culture of Seventeenth-Century Politics* (Cambridge: Cambridge University Press, 2000), 51; David Schalkwyk, *Shakespeare, Love and Service* (Cambridge: Cambridge University Press, 2008), 19.

[67] Gouge, *Of Domesticall Duties*, sig. B3ʳ.

Is now become the steward of his house, | And bravely jets it in his silken gown' (1.26–9).

Given the centrality of service and its language to early modern culture, it is not surprising that *Arden* should be suffused with the language of service, denoting the most benign acts of delivering a letter or making a bed as well as the most sinister: Mosby praising the painter, Clarke, for preparing the poison which will be used in Master Arden's broth ('you served me well' (1.245)). Even the play's masterless men, Black Will and Shakebag, who stand outside and in opposition to the community's values by virtue of their vagrancy and criminality (they dream at one point of murder becoming a respectable occupation so 'that a man might work without danger of law'), employ the language of service when greeting the play's most socially elevated character, Lord Cheyney: 'God save your honour. | I am your beadsman, bound to pray for you', 'bound' being a common way of describing the status of servants in the period (9.119–20).

Arden is concerned with exploring the consequences of bad household government for the relationships between employers and domestic servants, tracing the impact of domestic disorder on Michael and Susan, the Ardens' household servants. Collapsing two historical figures, Mosby's sister, Cisleye Ponder, and the Ardens' maidservant, Elsabeth Stafford, into one, Susan, and drastically reducing the number of servants employed by the Ardens, the play produces a household which is at once claustrophobic and fragmented. While Susan and Michael (the historical servant's name is Mighell Saunderson) are the only two servants employed by the Ardens in the play, they do not exchange any lines until after the murder, and Michael has to content himself with his mistress being a mediator between them and to resort to a letter to be sent from London to his beloved. Both servants are recruited into Mistress Arden's murder plans, the former at the outset in exchange for Susan's hand in marriage; the latter after the fact when she is ordered first to clean the bloodstains left by her master's body on the floor, then to help convey his body out of the house. Despite the involvement of servants in this murder, in the period servants were more likely to be the victims of domestic murder than its perpetrators.[68]

[68] J. S. Cockburn, 'The Nature and Incidence of Crime in England, 1559–1525: A Preliminary Survey', in J. S. Cockburn (ed.), *Crime in England 1550–1800* (London: Methuen, 1977), 57.

This is hardly surprising given the fact that violence was built into this relationship in the form of 'correction', that is, physical punishment. A household master and mistress had the right to discipline ill-behaved servants, within reasonable limits. However, fatal violence did sometimes occur, and the exact meaning of 'reasonable' correction remained vague. As did master- and mistress-murder.

Given the nature of the transgression embedded in those murders, like husband-murder, master-murder received attention out of proportion with its actual occurrence. Pamphlets reporting murders by servants often employ common tropes and draw on established formulas for representing murderous servants. Anxieties revealed in those accounts revolve around the physical proximity of servants to their employers, their familiarity with the domestic map, and the privileged knowledge to which such proximity and familiarity give them access. Common tropes include the sense of treachery, of the violation of trust and of the proprieties of domestic space as well as of household relationships. Narratives of master-murder often employ strategies to manage the anxieties raised by the figure of the murderous servant, such as recording the arrest, repentance, and punishment of those figures, thus reassuring their readers that order is restored. Accounts sometimes also strip the servants of their agency by suggesting that they were inspired by the devil. An example of this appears on the title-page woodcut of *Horrible Cruel and Bloody Murther Committed at Putney* (1614), where the devil is depicted egging on a murderous, axe-wielding servant while his master sleeps on unaware of the betrayal.

Following his recruitment into his mistress's murder plot, Michael's characterization as a murderous servant resonates closely with those tropes and evokes similar anxieties. Critic Frances E. Dolan has explored the way servants were seen as 'dangerous familiars', that is, as insiders who, by virtue of their status as 'outsider[s] within', their inside knowledge of their masters' intimate affairs, 'habits and vulnerabilities', constituted a source of threat to their masters and mistresses.[69] The danger Michael poses to his master revolves around his insider knowledge and proximity. For example, he uses the intimate knowledge he has access to through his service relationship to his

[69] Frances E. Dolan, 'The Subordinate('s) Plot: Petty Treason and the Forms of Domestic Rebellion', *Shakespeare Quarterly*, 43/3 (1992), 324–5.

master to facilitate the assassins' murderous task. Like any other servant, Michael knows his master's whereabouts, his routines and habits, and has access to his diary. He is ready with information about his master's personal activities whenever questioned: 'My master hath new supped, | And I am going to prepare his chamber'; '[my master supped] At the Nag's Head, at the eighteen-pence ordinary' (3.120–1, 123).

Further anxieties triggered by Michael's murderous service cluster around a trusted servant's duty to lock doors and guard entrances and exits to the house. Betraying his duty, Michael agrees to let the hired assassins enter his master's dwelling in London, familiarizing them with the domestic map: 'This night come to his house at Aldersgate. | The doors I'll leave unlocked against you come. | No sooner shall ye enter through the latch, | Over the threshold to the inner court, | But on your left hand shall you see the stairs | That leads directly to my master's chamber' (3.173–8). The anxiety surrounding servants' privileged access finds its fullest expression in the murder scene when, as murderers take positions around the parlour where Master Arden will be killed, Michael's role increasingly revolves around doors. The duty to lock doors which Michael failed to perform earlier on now gets performed, but with a twist which captures the perversion of service in this disordered household. In the lead-up to the murder, Michael is trusted by his mistress to lock doors, in effect turning the house into a trap from which the victim cannot escape. 'When my husband is come in,' Mistress Arden instructs her servant, 'lock the street door; | He shall he be murdered ere the guests come in' (14.163–4). In the aftermath of the murder, Michael will continue to be associated with doors, his service perverting the purposes of trusting a servant to lock doors. If locking doors ensured the household's safety during the night against forces of disorder imagined as active outside it, Michael's action of locking doors against the Mayor and the Watch, as his mistress instructs him to do (358), aims at protecting the forces of disorder active *within* the house (the murderers who have just committed their crime) and hindering the course of justice whose representatives are thus shut out. Similarly, Michael's service is perverted in the murder scene through Mistress Arden's staging of the scene. Michael, she decides, will 'stand before the counting-house door' for, she explains, 'Black Will is locked within to do the deed' (14.154, 156). Michael's usual duty to attend on his master's nocturnal activities, convivial and culinary, is being repurposed here into a darker version that has him attending on those waiting for the right moment to murder his master.

While the sentence of hanging passed on Michael at the end of the play records the actual punishment of the Ardens' servant, it is instructive that the play adopts another strategy to manage the threat of the murderous servant. Among the murderers, Michael is the only one who expresses hesitation and experiences a conflict of loyalties. Michael delivers two soliloquies in which he struggles with his divided loyalties, his duty towards his master, his fear of the assassins, and his love for Susan, the woman, his mistress has convinced him, he can only obtain through murdering his master. Summing up the different sides to a battle he visualizes himself as fighting internally, Michael lists them clearly: 'My master's kindness pleads to me for life', 'My mistress she hath forced me with an oath | For Susan's sake, the which I may not break', 'That grim-faced fellow, pitiless Black Will, | And Shakebag, stern in bloody stratagem… | Have sworn my death if I infringe my vow, | A dreadful thing to be considered of' (4.62–71). The play even registers his shock at witnessing his mistress stab his master: 'O, mistress!', he cries almost getting himself killed for his pains (14.235). By staging Michael's sentencing to death and blaming his murderous service on Mistress Arden's machinations and manipulations (Michael is emphatic that he has no personal grudge against his master, describing him as a blameless 'lamb', a sacrificial victim, in 3.185), *Arden* manages anxieties raised by the prospect of murderous service even as it highlights the consequences of wifely rebellion for the entire household and community.

'listen to the sentence I shall give': Justice

Arden of Faversham, and the genre of domestic tragedy generally, has long been perceived as didactic in purpose. The genre's first serious critic, Henry Hitch Adams, argued that the plays should be viewed as 'homiletic' in nature, explaining that they share the same goal as the medieval morality plays: 'Elizabethan domestic tragedies inculcated lessons of morality and religious faith in the citizens who came to the theatres.'[70] The fact that those plays feature the trajectory of murderers

[70] Henry Hitch Adams, *English Domestic or Homiletic Tragedy, 1575–1642* (New York: Columbia University Press, 1943), viii.

from planning their crimes to executing them, then to inevitable discovery, apprehension, and execution, has facilitated such readings. Moreover, the origin of most domestic tragedies in moralizing literature, such as murder pamphlets, suggests a shared vision. *Arden*'s own title-page sets up expectation about a moralistic tale, promising to show 'the shameful end of all murderers'. The play certainly taps into the discourse of divine providence when, for example, snow suddenly starts to fall when the murderers drag their victim's body into the fields, resulting in the detection of their footprints later on (14.391–2). Similarly, Master Arden's corpse starts bleeding in the presence of his murderer in an enactment of cruentation, the belief that the lifeless body of a murder victim bleeds when touched by its murderer, incriminating them ('This blood condemns me, and in gushing forth | Speaks as it falls and asks me why I did it', observes Mistress Arden (16.5–6)). The 'foggy mist' which interrupts the murder attempt in scene 12 could also be seen as an example of divine providence, allowing Master Arden to escape unharmed and landing one of his would-be murderers in a ditch.

However, this reading of domestic tragedies as didactic in purpose has been challenged since. For example, since many of those plays were based on contemporary murders, they would have appealed to their audiences as thrillers.[71] Peter Ure has argued that writers of domestic tragedy 'had to handle character and incident before an audience' and, therefore, they 'should be judged as dramatists and not as homilists'.[72] The moral message of domestic tragedies, if that is what it is, is certainly far from straightforward, and *Arden* is no exception. On the one hand, the play represents Master Arden as a morally ambiguous figure, even suggesting in the Epilogue that his death is punishment for his greed and lack of charity symbolized by his harsh treatment of the Reede family: 'Arden lay murdered in that plot of ground | Which he by force and violence held from Reede' (10–11). This comes straight from Holinshed who, despite opening his account of the murder by squarely placing the blame on the shoulders of Arden's wicked wife, writes in a marginal gloss that Arden's death

[71] Madeleine Doran, *Endeavors of Art: A Study of Form in Elizabethan Drama* (Madison: University of Wisconsin Press, 1954), 143.

[72] Peter Ure, 'Marriage and Domestic Drama in *A Woman Killed with Kindness*', in Max Bluestone and Norman Rabkin (eds), *Shakespeare's Contemporaries: Modern Studies in English Renaissance Drama* (Englewood Cliffs, NJ: Prentice-Hall, 1970), 197.

shows that 'God heareth the tears of the oppressed and takes vengeance', imploring the reader to 'note an example in Arden'.[73] Seen from this angle, Mistress Arden's murder of her husband looks like the fulfilment of a divine retributive plan.

Also undermining the didactic message of the play is the conventional nature of Mistress Arden's repentance speech delivered over the body of her dead husband in scene 16. Given her characterization as a consummate performer throughout the play, it is not far-fetched to see her repentance speech as yet another performance devoid of genuine remorse.[74] The repentance speech certainly follows the conventional formula expected from convicted criminals: expressing her remorse ('I repent me now'), asking for forgiveness ('Forgive me, Arden'), and articulating hope in redemption ('when we meet in heaven') (16.7, 10). Instructively, Joan Littlewood's 1954 production of *Arden* at the Theatre Royal, Stratford East, London, excised Alice's speech of repentance completely, further complicating the supposedly didactic nature of the play and leaving her true feelings about the murder at the end inaccessible. The most serious challenge to the didacticism argument is the way the play's ending does not represent justice as operating fairly. Bradshaw, an innocent man whose involvement in the murder is restricted to delivering a letter to Mistress Arden from Master Greene following a failed attempt on her husband, is sentenced to death for his supposed complicity. As representatives of the judiciary system dismiss his desperate pleas for justice, he goes to his death cursing the system: 'My blood be on his head that gave the sentence!' (18.37). Similarly, Susan, despite only learning of the crime after it has been performed, is sentenced to being burnt alive as a petty traitor. Her pleas for mercy go similarly unheeded, and her resignation to her unjust fate ('Seeing no hope on earth, in heaven is my hope' (18.35)) is a culmination of her victimization and helplessness throughout the play. On the other hand, Clarke, the painter and provider of poison, manages to flee justice: 'The painter fled, and how he died we know not' (Epilogue 8). The Richmond Shakespeare Society 2024 production spatially reproduced this injustice by setting the play 'in hell'. Presided over by The Guide in

[73] In Wine (ed.), *The Tragedy of Arden of Faversham*, 159.

[74] Cheryl Birdseye, '"Let death make amends for all my sins": (In)Sincere Confessions in *Arden of Faversham*', *Early Modern Literary Studies*, Special Issue 28 (2019), 1–22.

Hell, all the characters, regardless of the nature or degree of their involvement in the crime, stood in line at the back of the stage, their punishment, the end of the production reveals, consisting of replaying their roles *ad infinitum*.

The nature of drama, the fact that transgression is first staged and experienced, motives explored, and disobedience articulated before attempts at containment are made in the final scene, means that the audience is exposed to ideas which cannot be easily erased when the performance ends. For example, Mistress Arden's chafing at her contradictory position in her household as both mistress invested with domestic, social, and spiritual authority over her children and servants, and subordinate to her husband would have spoken to the lived realities of many female playgoers. Some aspects of her plight, therefore, might have felt relatable and received sympathy from at least those members of the audience.[75] We do have evidence that early modern women did not necessarily passively accept or internalize the tenets of patriarchy delineated in oral and print culture. The preacher William Gouge admitted in his highly influential treatise *Of Domesticall Duties* (1622) that whenever he instructed his parishioners in 'the doctrine of female submission and inferiority', he felt 'a certain amount of squirming and murmuring on the part of the women in the audience'.[76] Such comments suggest that preachers were more involved in prescribing than describing and that, despite their claims for the 'naturalness' of the gender hierarchy placing women under men, they were aware that there was nothing 'natural' about this social arrangement. In fact, audience reception and interpretation was one of the aspects over which both defenders and opponents of the theatre clashed in the period. Thus Thomas Heywood, the author of the domestic tragedy *A Woman Killed with Kindness*, argued in a work which defended the theatre that plays 'comprehend... what in our lives and manners is to be followed, what to be avoided'. The author of an anti-theatrical work, *Refutation of the Apology for Actors* (1615), however, opposed this view, instead declaring that: 'Stage-players... to please the vulgar... set before them lies, and teach them

[75] For women as playgoers, see Andrew Gurr, *Playgoing in Shakespeare's London* (Cambridge: Cambridge University Press, 1987), 55–63.

[76] Cited in Viviana Comensoli, *Household Business: Domestic Plays of Early Modern England* (Toronto: University of Toronto Press, 1996), 21.

much dissolution and deceitfulness', for they teach 'how in our lives and manners we may follow all kinds of vice with art'.[77] Mistress Arden's bid to 'rule myself' (10.85), Bradshaw's indictment of the unjust judiciary system, and Susan's lament ('wherefore should I die?' (18.19)), cannot be easily silenced or erased by the ending of the play, regardless of whether or not the playwrights wished to deliver a didactic message.

Shakespeare and Domestic Tragedy

The first time the play was associated with Shakespeare was in the mid-seventeenth century when the bookseller Edward Archer seems to have intended to place Shakespeare's name next to *Arden*. The next attribution to Shakespeare had to wait until 1770 when Edward Jacob, a local historian of Faversham, published an edition of the play, describing it as 'the earliest dramatic Work of Shakespear now remaining', based on verbal similarities between the play and Shakespeare's other plays.[78] Recent discussions of *Arden*'s authorship have built on Jacob's work, improving his methods by making use of computational stylistics tests which compare particular passages from the play with the work of potential playwrights and produce a hierarchy of possible authors. Based on such tests, proposed candidates for the authorship of *Arden* have included Christopher Marlowe, Thomas Kyd, Thomas Watson, and, of course, Shakespeare.

While Shakespeare did not write a play which fits perfectly the characteristics which have come to be associated with the genre (the relatively humble social origins of its protagonists, the domestic nature of its concerns, the themes of marital strife and household disorder it tackles), many of his plays share thematic concerns, elements, and tropes with the genre. *Othello*'s focus on the marital problems of Othello and Desdemona, its exploration of jealousy and of the potential conflict between male friendship and heterosexual relationships, and its staging of domestic violence and a wife's murder has led at

[77] Thomas Heywood, *An Apology for Actors* (1612), sig. F1^{v}; I. G., *A Refutation of the Apology for Actors* (London: W. White, 1615), sig. F1^{r}.

[78] W. W. Greg, 'Shakespeare and *Arden of Feversham*', *Review of English Studies*, 21/82 (1945), 134–6; Edward Jacob (ed.), *The Lamentable and True Tragedie of M. Arden, of Feversham, in Kent* (Faversham: J & J March, 1770), iii.

least one critic to call for its inclusion within the genre.[79] More recently, critic Emma Whipday has argued that Shakespeare's plays often literalize the metaphorical analogy between household and state on which many domestic tragedies depend to stage the consequences of domestic disorder.[80] This is, for example, seen in *Macbeth* where Duncan is king, guest, and kinsman, someone owed allegiance and hospitality at the same time: 'He's here in double trust: | First as I am his kinsman and his subject, | . . . then as his host, | Who should against his murderer shut the door, | Not bear the knife myself', agonizes Macbeth.[81] Echoes of the Ardens' servant Michael's conflicted conscience and sense of betrayed responsibility closely resonate with Macbeth's: 'I, that should take the weapon in my hand | And buckler thee from ill-intending foes, | Do lead thee with a wicked, fraudful smile, | As unsuspected, to the slaughterhouse' (3.192–5). Similarly, in *King Lear*, Lear is both father and king; the domestic is also the state. In *Hamlet*, fratricide (killing a brother), akin to Michael's plan in *Arden*, is also regicide (killing a monarch). In those plays, petty treason is always also high treason, and the fragile boundary between the private and the public, which delusional characters such as Mistress Arden futilely try to enforce, does not exist.

Making the political nature of the household explicit, Shakespeare also stresses the domestic nature of politics. Arguably, the state sought to model itself on the domestic, the king's authority on that of the father, so as to suggest that such authority is natural, immutable, and beyond questioning.[82] By fusing the figures of the tyrannical father and the tyrannical ruler, as he does in *King Lear*, for example, Shakespeare explores the nature of power and exposes its vulnerability to abuse in domestic as well as in political settings. As such, he turns the early modern state's attempt to naturalize itself through analogy to the father's rule over his dependants on its head. *King Lear*'s questioning of fathers' tyranny through its depiction of both Lear and Gloucester, in a similar way to *Arden*'s questioning of a brother's right to dispose of his sister as suits his own selfish,

[79] Sean Benson, *Shakespeare, Othello, and Domestic Tragedy* (London: Bloomsbury, 2012).

[80] Whipday, *Shakespeare's Domestic Tragedies*, 4.

[81] William Shakespeare, *Macbeth*, ed. John Jowett in *The New Oxford Shakespeare: The Complete Works, Modern Critical Edition*, 1.7.12–16.

[82] Orlin, 'Domestic Tragedy: Private Life on the Public Stage', 373.

murderous purposes, renders the political authority those characters embody (Lear, literally; Mosby, analogically) also open to question and critique. By staging stories immediately recognizable to the original audiences and relevant to their lived experiences as spouses, masters and mistresses, servants, siblings, and neighbours, Shakespeare's use of domestic tragedy in his more overtly political plays demystifies politics and invites audience engagement and judgement on the political stories they witness, which are at their heart also domestic stories. In literalizing the interdependability between the home and the state, Shakespeare invites his audience to confront the possibility that political authority is neither unchangeable nor metaphysically ordained either.

NOTE ON THE TEXT

Arden was published before the other collaborative plays that dominate the beginning of Shakespeare's career: *Titus Andronicus*, the three parts of *Henry VI*, and *Edward III*. It was registered for publication on 3 April 1592. Its publication was authorized by the Bishop of London, the government censor. A blasphemous reference to 'the Lord of heauen' (9.143) almost certainly suffered censorship, which probably also affected the 'prayer book' passage (8.116–22) and 9.36.1.

Edward White—who specialized in 'true crime' genres—published *Arden* later that year, in an edition printed by Edward Allde (White's favourite printer). Allde specialized in cheap titles like ballads, chapbooks, jestbooks, pamphlets, and commercial plays, whose readers did not expect exceptional accuracy. His carelessness is evident in numerous mechanical errors, like 'entes' for 'enters' (1.56.1), corrected in this edition.

Allde worked from a manuscript that seems to have been prepared especially for publication. The text contains none of the sound cues or other features characteristic of theatrical manuscripts. Its stage directions are systematic, old-fashioned, and idiosyncratic: almost all entrance directions use the formula 'Here enters', and directions for onstage action (other than entrances or exits) all begin with 'Then'. Of the play's eighteen scenes, all conclude with an 'Exit' or 'Exeunt' direction, removing all the onstage characters (followed by a 'Here enters' direction, beginning the next scene). These features are not found in other publications by White, Allde, or Shakespeare, and they suggest some sort of literary transcript, prepared for a patron or specifically for sale. Any stage directions added by the New Oxford editors respect the system used in the first edition.

The play's title creates insoluble editorial difficulties. Whose tragedy is it? The play contains two characters surnamed 'Arden', and for both of them the first edition uses the ambiguous abbreviation 'M.' (meaning modern 'Mr' or 'Mrs'). The wife is indisputably the dominant character, speaking 4,840 words, almost exactly twice as many as her husband (2,438). This makes Alice the largest female tragic role in the Shakespeare canon. The dialogue identifies her as

'Mistress Arden' five times (1.450, 464, 469, 488, 546) before her husband is first identified as 'Master Arden'. In the play's beginning and ending, the status marker refers exclusively to the female Arden. Theatrically and textually, the tragedy of 'M. Arden' is a woman's tragedy.

That tragedy happens in a town now called 'Faversham'. But in the first edition, both Master and Mistress Arden are 'of Feuershame' (='Fevershame'). The running titles consistently specify 'Arden of Feuershame', and the text has 'Feuershame' thirteen times. That unusual spelling is also found in John Stow's unpublished sixteenth-century manuscript account of Arden's murder (a possible source for the play), entitled 'The history of a most horrible murder comytyd at ffevershame in Kent'. The line 'In health towards Fevershame, to shame us all' (9.139) puns on both halves of the name: 'health' contrasts with 'Fever', and the verb 'shame' clearly echoes the name's final syllable. Reluctantly, our modern-spelling edition modernizes to 'Faversham'.

Notes in this text are derived from the *New Oxford Shakespeare*. That edition is a collaborative work and for full acknowledgement of all the scholars involved please refer to that publication.

Terri Bourus

SELECT BIBLIOGRAPHY

The Oxford World's Classics depend on the extraordinary editorial labours of the *New Oxford Shakespeare* team, who, under the leadership of Gary Taylor, John Jowett, Terri Bourus, and Gabriel Egan, have rethought details large and small about these texts. Readers are encouraged to explore the resources of that edition, and to refer to *The New Oxford Shakespeare: Modern Critical Edition* (Oxford: Oxford University Press, 2016) for further information. All references to other works by Shakespeare in the introduction and notes to this edition are taken from the *New Oxford Shakespeare*.

General Reading

De Grazia, Margreta, and Stanley Wells, eds, *The New Cambridge Companion to Shakespeare* (Cambridge: Cambridge University Press, 2010).

Gajowski, Evelyn, ed., *The Arden Research Handbook of Contemporary Shakespeare Criticism* (London: Bloomsbury, 2022).

Karim-Cooper, Farah, *The Great White Bard: How to Love Shakespeare while Talking about Race* (London: Simon and Schuster, 2023).

McEvoy, Sean, *Shakespeare: The Basics* (London: Taylor and Francis, 2006).

Orlin, Lena Cowen, *The Private Life of William Shakespeare* (Oxford: Oxford University Press, 2021).

Smith, Emma, *This Is Shakespeare* (London: Pelican, 2019).

Smuts, Malcolm, ed., *The Oxford Handbook of the Age of Shakespeare* (Oxford: Oxford University Press, 2018).

On Arden of Faversham *and Domestic Tragedy*

Belsey, Catherine, *The Subject of Tragedy: Identity and Difference in Renaissance Drama* (London: Methuen, 1985).

Comensoli, Viviana, *Household Business: Domestic Plays of Early Modern England* (Toronto: University of Toronto Press, 1996).

Dolan, Frances E., 'Home-Rebels and House-Traitors: Murderous Wives in Early Modern England', *Yale Journal of Law & the Humanities*, 4/1 (1992), 1–31.

Kirwan, Peter and Duncan Salkeld (eds), *Arden of Faversham: A Critical Reader* (London: Bloomsbury, 2023).

Orlin, Lena Cowen, *Private Matters and Public Culture in Post-Reformation England* (Ithaca, NY and London: Cornell University Press, 1994).

Richardson, Catherine, *Domestic Life and Domestic Tragedy in Early Modern England: The Material Life of the Household* (Manchester: Manchester University Press, 2013).

Whipday, Emma, *Shakespeare's Domestic Tragedies: Violence in the Early Modern Home* (Cambridge: Cambridge University Press, 2019).

A CHRONOLOGY OF WILLIAM SHAKESPEARE

1564	(26 Apr.) William Shakespeare, third child of John Shakespeare (a glover) and Mary Arden, is baptized.
1569	Shakespeare probably attends King's New School.
	Northern Rebellion.
1582	(27–8 Nov.) Shakespeare, still a minor, and Anne Hathaway, pregnant, file for a marriage licence.
1583	(26 May) First child, Susanna, is christened.
1584	First attempted English settlement in America (Roanoke).
1585	(2 Feb.) Hamnet and Judith, twins, are christened.
c.1587	*The Two Gentlemen of Verona* likely written. An earlier draft may have been performed in Stratford-upon-Avon, and some elements may have been revised mid-1590s.
1587	*Holinshed's Chronicles* (2nd edition), source for Shakespeare's history plays.
1588	(Aug.) Defeat of Spanish Armada.
c.1592	Shakespeare moves to London some time before 1592. *Groatsworth of Wit* (Robert Greene, 1592) contains the thinly veiled first reference to Shakespeare on the theatrical scene ('an upstart crow'), and alludes to *Henry VI, Part III* ('tiger's heart wrapped in a players hide'). Contains potential allusions to plagiarism, and attacks him for his actor credentials.
	Henry VI, Part I is performed by Lord Strange's Men. Shakespeare identified as author of 2.4, 4.2, and parts of 4.3–4.5, probably later additions (maybe added 1594–5). Also includes work by Nashe and Marlowe.
	Likely composition date of *Edward III*. Though published anonymously, attribution scholars suggest Shakespeare wrote part of scenes 2, 3, and 12.
1592	*Arden of Faversham* first published (anonymously). Many critics agree Shakespeare had a hand in scenes 4–8, and dispute scene 9.

Playhouses are shut for the plague, opening for a short season in Dec. 1593–Feb. 1594, closing again after that.

1592–3 Likely composition of *Sir Thomas More*, originally written by Munday and Chettle. It was revised by several writers, probably around 1603–4, including a three-page handwritten revision attributed to Shakespeare.

1593 (18 Apr.) *Venus and Adonis* is registered in the Stationers' Register. Printed as a quarto, and relatively free of errors, it suggests the competence of printer Richard Field.

1594 Short version of *Henry VI, Part II*, 'The first part of the Contention of the Two Famous Houses of York and Lancaster, with the Death of the good Duke Humphrey', is published. Authorship contested: Shakespeare securely identified as the author of Act 3 and Young Clifford's speech.

The Taming of a Shrew, a text with radical differences from *The Taming of the Shrew*, is printed. The familiar version would not be printed until 1623.

(6 Feb.) *Titus Andronicus* is registered with the Stationers' Register. On 24 Jan., Henslowe records the performance of the play by Sussex's Men as 'new'. New can, however, mean recently licensed or republished: it was likely written between 1584 and 1594.

(9 May) *The Ravishment of Lucrece* is registered in the Stationers' Register, printed by Field. It is dedicated to the Earl of Southampton, Shakespeare's patron.

(Summer) Lord Chamberlain's Men formed.

(28 Dec.) *The Comedy of Errors* is performed at Gray's Inn, to tumult and disorder. Becomes known as the Night of Errors.

1595 Likely date of composition of *Richard II*.

Henry VI, Part III (which was created by 1592) is printed as an octavo, titled 'The True Tragedie of Richard Duke of York, and the Death of Good King Henrie the Sixt'.

1596 Thomas Lodge recalls an early *Hamlet*, in which the lines 'Hamlet, revenge!' feature.

First edition of *Edward III*, which had 'been sundry times played about the City of London'.

Likely composition date of *King John*.

(11 Aug.) Hamnet dies aged 11, and is buried in the churchyard of Holy Trinity, Stratford.

*c.*1597 Francis Mere's *Palladis Tamia*, 'Wit's Treasury. Being the Second Part of Wit's Common Wealth', references twelve plays as belonging to Shakespeare: *Gentlemen of Verona*, *Comedy of Errors*, *Love's Labour's Lost*, *Love's Labour Won*, *A Midsummer Night's Dream*, *Merchant of Venice*, *Richard II* & *III*, *Henry IV*, *King John*, *Titus Andronicus*, and *Romeo and Juliet*.

1597 *Romeo and Juliet* published.

Shakespeare buys a house on 'New Place', on Chapel Street, the second largest in Stratford.

Richard II first appears as a quarto edition.

Richard III is published in a quarto.

(13 Apr.) James Burbage's lease on the Theatre expires, and he purchases Blackfriars' Monastery. However, the aristocratic residents of the area complain to the Privy Council, preventing the company from moving in.

(July) After a salacious performance at the Swan, the Privy Council assents to the Lord Mayor and Alderman's petition for the surpressing of stage plays, and further orders the dismantling of Shoreditch and Bankside theatres, including the Theatre. However, this is not final, and the Theatre ends up reopening.

James Burbage dies.

(Christmas period) *Love's Labour's Lost*, and two other plays, are performed before Queen Elizabeth. The company is paid £40.

1598 Second Quarto of *Richard II* and *III* published, now bearing Shakespeare's name. *Love's Labour's Lost* is also published 'by W. Shakespere'—first extant copy, but self-described as 'Newly Corrected and Augmented'.

Henry IV, Part I is newly published in quarto, printed with 'Falstaff' rather than 'Oldcastle', under pressure from the Cobham family, descendants of the historical Oldcastle.

(28 Dec.) Unable to secure a lease with the landlord of the Theatre, Giles Allen and the Burbage brothers, along with a team of builders, disassemble the Theatre under the cover of darkness, ship the timber across to Bankside, and erect the Globe.

1598–9 (Christmas period) The Chamberlain's Men play twice in court.

1599 (21 Feb.) Globe agreement drawn up as a tripartite lease, with Shakespeare, as part of the Chamberlain's Men, owning 1/10th of the shares.

(*c.* Feb.) 'To the Queen', composed for a court performance, written. Stylometric evidence suggests it is Shakespeare's work.

(Mar.) Essex leaves for Ireland with 16,000 troops, returning in Sept., a failure.

Second, longer (still anonymous) version of *Romeo and Juliet* is published with a title-page claiming that it is 'Newly corrected, augmented, amended'.

Likely composition date of *Julius Caesar.*

Third edition of *Henry IV, Part I* is published, including Shakespeare's name for the first time.

The Passionate Pilgrim (two editions) is published as a pamphlet in octavo format. The title-page attributes the work to Shakespeare, though only five poems can be certainly attributed to him. Five of the poems would later appear in Shakespeare's *Sonnets* (138 and 144) and *Love's Labour's Lost.* It includes poems by Richard Barnfield, Thomas Deloney, Christopher Marlowe, Walter Raleigh, and Bartholomew Griffin.

1599–1600 Chamberlain's Men perform twice at court over the Christmas period.

1600 *The Merchant of Venice* first published.

First quarto of *Much Ado About Nothing.*

Likely date of composition of *As You Like It.*

Likely date of composition of *The Merry Wives of Windsor.*

A Midsummer's Night's Dream is printed in quarto.

Henry IV, Part II is printed in quarto.

Henry V is printed in quarto, as a corrupted shortened text.

1600–1 Chamberlain's Men perform twice at court over the Christmas period.

1601 (7 Feb.) On the evening of the Essex Rebellion, supporters of the Earl of Essex request a performance of *Richard II.* The Lord Chamberlain's Men brought in for questioning by the Privy Council.

(8 Feb.) Essex rebellion. The Earl of Essex makes a bid for power, marching on court (unsuccessfully), before marching back through the city, barricading himself in Essex House, and finally surrendering. Southampton, Shakespeare's patron, escapes with imprisonment.

(8 Sept.) John Shakespeare buried, the house on Henley Street passing on to William Shakespeare.

Probable date of composition of *Twelfth Night*. John Manningham attends a performance of the play at the Middle Temple on the Feast of Candlemas, 1602.

1601–2 Chamberlain's Men perform three times at court over the Christmas period.

1602 *Sir John Falstaff and The Merry Wives of Windsor* is first printed in quarto.

The intent to publish 'The Tragicall Historie of Hamlet Prince of Denmarke' is entered in the Stationers' Register, though the 'first quarto' will not be printed until autumn 1603.

1603 Date of printing of *Hamlet* first quarto (earliest extant copy).

(2 Feb.) Chamberlain's Men play for the last time before the queen.

(7 Feb.) *Troilus and Cressida* entered in the Stationers' Register, likely composed 1602. It is not, however, printed until 1609.

(24 Mar.) Queen dies and her 'kinsman, the King of Scots' James VI / I ascends to the throne.

(17 May) Troupe becomes the King's Men.

1604 (Jan.) Private production of *Love's Labour's Lost* staged by the King's Men, at Southamption or Cecil House.

Likely composition of *Othello*, originally titled *The Moor of Venice*.

(1 Nov.) *Othello* (stage name 'The Moor of Venice') first performed at court on Hallowmas Day.

(26 Dec.) *Measure for Measure* performed in front of the new king and court at the Banqueting House at Whitehall.

(28 Dec.) *The Comedy of Errors* performed for King James.

1604–5 Printing of second, longer quarto of *Hamlet*, over the New Year (hence, some dated 1604 (3 copies), others 1605 (4 copies)).

1605 *All's Well That Ends Well* probable composition date. Adapted by Middleton most likely around 1621. First recorded performance 1741.

(Feb.) *The Merchant of Venice* performed at court twice in three days.

1606 Most likely composition date of *Timon of Athens*.

Original composition date of *Macbeth*. Adapted a decade later with Thomas Middleton. May have been staged at the court of James I as well as the Globe.

(26 Dec.) Shakespeare's *King Lear* performed at court.

Master of Revels now able to license plays for print.

Likely date of composition of *Antony and Cleopatra*; first performed around 1607.

1607 Virginia Company, chartered by 1606, founds Jamestown colony.

(26 Nov.) *King Lear* entered on the Stationers' Register. The First Quarto printed 1608, giving the longest and earliest text.

1608 New edition of *Richard II* includes new deposition scene.

The King's Men reassume the lease of Blackfriars from Henry Evans.

Mary Arden, Shakespeare's mother, dies.

Likely composition of *Coriolanus*. There were no recorded performances during Shakespeare's lifetime. However, possible allusions can be found in *c.*1609 by Robert Armin and Ben Jonson. The first confirmed performance was Nahum Tate's 1681 adaptation.

1609 *Pericles* is first published (likely written around 1608), and reprinted frequently. First edition is very corrupted. First eleven scenes likely written by George Wilkins.

(28 Jan.) *Troilus and Cressida* is published under unusual circumstances, as a 'new play' 'never staled with the stage, never clapper-clawed by the hands of the vulgar'. It was likely only new to readers. It was originally submitted to the Stationers' Register six years prior, but it was never published. In 1609, Bonian and Walley entered it on the register as written by William Shakespeare and acted by His Majesty's Servants at the Globe.

	Thomas Thorpe publishes a quarto edition of the *Sonnets*. Some had circulated since at least 1599 in *The Passionate Pilgrim*.
	King's Men assume operations at Blackfriars, primarily using it as their winter theatre.
1610	Likely composition of *Cymbeline*.
*c.*1609/11	Likely composition of *The Winter's Tale.*
1611	Likely composition of *The Tempest*, the last play Shakespeare composed alone.
	Simon Forman describes seeing *Macbeth* (20 Apr.), and *The Winter's Tale* (15 May) at the Globe, and also *Cymbeline* (no date or theatre listed).
1612	(May) Shakespeare gives evidence at the Court of Requests, in London.
	Likely date of *Henry VIII* ('All is True') composition, with Fletcher. Shakespeare would also collaborate with Fletcher on *Cardenio* and his likely final play, *The Two Noble Kinsmen*.
1613	(Feb.) King's Men perform at Whitehall for the nuptials of Princess Elizabeth and Prince Frederick, performing fourteen plays including *Much Ado About Nothing*, *Othello*, *The Winter's Tale*, and *The Tempest*. Paid £93 6s. 8d.
	(Mar.) Shakespeare buys a home in the Blackfriars' Constituency, London, for £140. At some point between 1610 and 1613, however, Shakespeare has moved back to Stratford.
	(29 Jun.) *Henry VIII* performed at the Globe, probably written *c.*1612. During the performance, and as noted by Sir Henry Wotton, a theatrical cannon misfired and caught the thatch. Within a year a new Globe, with a tiled roof, was built on the same site.
1613–14	Likely date of composition of *The Two Noble Kinsmen*, probably written with Fletcher.
1616	(25 Mar.) Shakespeare summons his lawyer, Francis Collins, and makes his last Will and Testament. The will was possibly drafted in Jan., and revised in Mar. to reflect Judith's marital status. The will is typical of a Jacobean man of means, although it is light on philanthropy.
	(23 Apr.) Shakespeare dies, aged 52. He is buried at Holy Trinity Church, Stratford-upon-Avon.

1618 (Easter Monday) Performance of *Twelfth Night* at court.

1622 *The Tragedy of Othello* printed in quarto (as a shorter text). Claims that Shakespeare's 'name is enough' to sell any play.

1623 The First Folio, 'Comedies, Histories, & Tragedies', a collection of thirty-six plays, is published. Compiled by Shakespeare's fellow actors and friends John Heminges and Henry Condell.

1634 Publication of quarto text of *The Two Noble Kinsmen*, attributed to Shakespeare and John Fletcher on the title-page.

THE TRAGEDY OF M. ARDEN OF FAVERSHAM; OR, THE TRAGEDY OF M. ARDEN OF FEVERSHAME

title M. This abbreviation may be used for both 'Master' and 'Mistress' (the original forms of modern 'Mr' and 'Mrs', but in the sixteenth century suggesting a higher status).

title Faversham The modern spelling of a small town in Kent, where the historical murder of Arden took place.

title Fevershame A sixteenth-century spelling of the name, used throughout the original text of the play, which suggests an allegorical place of fever and shame.

THE ROLES IN THE PLAY

ARDEN, a gentleman of Faversham
ALICE ARDEN, his wife
FRANKLIN, Arden's counsellor and friend
MOSBY, Alice's lover
MICHAEL, servant in the Arden household, in love with Susan
SUSAN, Mosby's sister; Alice's maid
CLARKE, a painter in love with Susan
Richard GREENE, a tenant whose land Arden has taken
Black WILL, a former soldier, now a professional criminal and killer
SHAKEBAG, Black Will's partner in crime

ADAM Fowle, landlord of the Flower-de-Luce, an inn in Faversham
BRADSHAW, a goldsmith (also a former soldier)
LORD CHEYNE of Kent, Arden's friend and patron
A FERRYMAN
Dick REEDE, a mariner from Faversham
A SAILOR, Reede's companion
The MAYOR of Faversham

A PRENTICE of a shop in London

Lord Cheyne's men, the Watch in Faversham, a London crowd

ARDEN OF FEVERSHAME

Sc. 1

Enter Arden and Franklin [with deeds]

FRANKLIN *Arden,* cheer up thy spirits and droop no more.
My gracious lord, the Duke of *Somerset,*
Hath freely given to thee and to thy heirs,
By letters patents from his majesty,
All the lands of the Abbey of *Faversham.*
Here are the deeds, sealed and subscribed with his name and the King's.
Read them, and leave this melancholy mood.

ARDEN Franklin, thy love prolongs my weary life—
And but for thee, how odious were this life,
That shows me nothing but torments my soul,
And those foul objects that offend mine eyes,
Which makes me wish that, for this veil of heaven,
The earth hung over my head and covered me.
Love letters passed 'twixt *Mosby* and my wife,
And they have privy meetings in the town.

Sc. 1 1.1–7 **Arden...mood** This dialogue immediately foregrounds issues of social status by emphasizing the possession of property (rather than inherited titles) in relation to attitudes of superiority and authority.

1.2 **Duke of Somerset** Edward Seymour (1506–52), the Lord Protector (1547–9) of Protestant King Edward VI when he was a child. Seymour was executed for treason in 1552.

1.4 **letters patents** (an official document issued by the government, usually conferring rights, property, or title to an individual)

1.4 **his majesty** i.e. Edward VI. The male pronoun would have established, for early audiences, that the action takes place before the reigns of Queen Mary and Queen Elizabeth.

1.5 **Abbey of Faversham** Henry VIII dissolved the abbey by indenture on 10 May 1540 and granted the land to Sir Thomas Cheyne (warden of the Cinque Ports) on 16 May 1540. The ownership of the land, tenements, and houses was transferred to Thomas Arden in 1547 by Cheyne (not Seymour).

1.6 **subscribed** signed

1.7 **melancholy** pensive, sad

1.10 **shows** provides

1.12 **for** instead of

1.12 **veil of heaven** sky, the celestial sphere

1.14 **'twixt** betwixt, between

1.15 **privy** private

Nay, on his finger did I spy the ring
Which at our marriage day the priest put on.
Can any grief be half so great as this?

FRANKLIN Comfort thyself, sweet friend: it is not strange
That women will be false and wavering.

ARDEN Ay, but to dote on such a one as he
Is monstrous, *Franklin*, and intolerable.

FRANKLIN Why, what is he?

ARDEN A botcher, and no better at the first,
Who, by base brokage getting some small stock,
Crept into service of a nobleman,
And by his servile flattery and fawning
Is now become the steward of his house,
And bravely jets it in his silken gown.

FRANKLIN No nobleman will count'nance such a peasant—

ARDEN Yes, the Lord Clifford, he that loves not me.
But through his favour let not him grow proud;
For were he by the Lord Protector backed,
He should not make me to be pointed at.
I am by birth a gentleman of blood,
And that injurious ribald that attempts
To violate my dear wife's chastity
(For dear I hold her love, as dear as heaven)
Shall on the bed which he thinks to defile
See his dissevered joints and sinews torn,

1.21 **dote on** adore, pamper
1.24–9 **A...gown** This speech is studded with language that underscores Mosby's inferior social standing.
1.24 **botcher** mender or patcher of clothing
1.24 **at the first** at his birth
1.25 **base brokage** brokerage, illegitimate business practices; activities as a panderer
1.25 **small stock** modest financial return
1.27 **fawning** obsequious behaviour
1.28 **steward** supervisor of the domestic activities in a household
1.29 **bravely jets** brazenly parades
1.29 **his silken gown** the *nobleman's* livery, i.e. the distinctive uniform worn by Lord Clifford's servants
1.30 **count'nance** support
1.31 **Lord Clifford** Henry Clifford (1517–70), 2nd Earl of Cumberland. A known Catholic sympathizer.
1.35 **I...blood** A *gentleman* was entitled to bear heraldic arms though not ranking among the nobility. Despite this claim, Arden's true status is uncertain (see 1.486–9) and it is possible that his newly acquired estate is what validates his identification as a member of the gentry.
1.36 **injurious** slanderous
1.36 **ribald** irreverent person
1.40 **dissevered** torn apart

Whilst on the planchers pants his weary body,
Smeared in the channels of his lustful blood.

FRANKLIN Be patient, gentle friend, and learn of me
To ease thy grief and save her chastity.
Entreat her fair; sweet words are fittest engines
To raze the flint walls of a woman's breast.
In any case be not too jealïous,
Nor make no question of her love to thee;
But, as securely, presently take horse
And lie with me at *London* all this term.
For women, when they may, will not,
But being kept back, straight grow outragëous.

ARDEN Though this abhors from reason, yet I'll try it,
And call her forth, and presently take leave.
How, Alice!

Here enters Alice

ALICE Husband, what mean you to get up so early?
Summer nights are short, and yet you rise ere day.
Had I been 'wake, you had not risse so soon.

ARDEN Sweet love, thou know'st that we two, *Ovid*-like,
Have often chid the morning when it 'gan to peep,
And often wished that dark Night's purblind steeds
Would pull her by the purple mantle back
And cast her in the ocean to her love.

1.41 **planchers** wooden floorboards, planks (i.e. gallows)
1.42 **channels** streams
1.45 **Entreat her fair** i.e. handle her delicately
1.45 **fittest engines** best devices
1.46 **raze** remove, scrape
1.46 **flint** hard stone
1.46 **breast** heart
1.49 **securely** confidently
1.50 **lie** stay, lodge
1.50 **term** (one of the four law-court sessions (Michaelmas, Hilary, Easter, Trinity) that divided the calendar year)
1.51–2 **For...outragëous** controlling women that do not wish to be restrained often causes them to behave in a disgraceful manner
1.53 **abhors** recoils from
1.58 **risse** risen
1.59–65 **Ovid-like...sleep** A translation of Ovid's Elegy 13 in Book 1 of the *Amores*: *Ad Auroram ne properet* (Do not hurry to the dawn). His thirteenth elegy urges the sun not to bring on the morning and end the night of love.
1.60 **chid** rebuked
1.61 **Night's purblind steeds** blind horses, alluding to Nyx the goddess of night who is often depicted as driving a chariot drawn by two horses
1.62 **her** the sun
1.62 **purple mantle** dark cloak
1.63 **the...love** In classical mythology, the sun was thought to spend every night with her lover, the ocean.

But this night, sweet *Alice,* thou hast killed my heart:
I heard thee call on Mosby in thy sleep.

ALICE 'Tis like I was asleep when I named him,
For being awake he comes not in my thoughts.

ARDEN Ay, but you started up and suddenly,
Instead of him, caught me about the neck.

ALICE 'Instead of him'? Why, who was there but you?
And where but one is, how can I mistake?

FRANKLIN Arden, leave to urge her overfar.

ARDEN [*to Alice*] Nay, love, there is no credit in a dream.
Let it suffice I know thou lov'st me well.

ALICE Now I remember whereupon it came:
Had we no talk of Mosby yesternight?

FRANKLIN Mistress Alice, I heard you name him once or twice.

ALICE And thereof came it, and therefore blame not me.

ARDEN I know it did, and therefore let it pass.
I must to London, sweet Alice, presently.

ALICE But tell me, do you mean to stay there long?

ARDEN No longer than till my affairs be done.

FRANKLIN He will not stay above a month at most.

ALICE A month? Ay me! Sweet Arden, come again
Within a day or two, or else I die.

ARDEN I cannot long be from thee, gentle Alice.
Whilst Michael fetch our horses from the field,
Franklin and I will down unto the quay,
For I have certain goods there to unload.
Meanwhile prepare our breakfast, gentle Alice,
For yet ere noon we'll take horse and away.

Exeunt Arden and Franklin

ALICE Ere noon he means to take horse and away!
Sweet news is this. O, that some airy spirit

1.66 **'Tis like** it is likely

1.70 **but you?** i.e. How could I be mistaken with only one person here?

1.72 **leave...overfar** refrain from pressing her too hard

1.73 **credit** truth, authenticity

1.75 **whereupon it came** how it came about

1.91 **ere** before

1.93 **airy spirit** vexatious fiend

Would in the shape and likeness of a horse
Gallop with Arden 'cross the ocëan
And throw him from his back into the waves!
Sweet Mosby is the man that hath my heart,
And he usurps it, having nought but this:
That I am tied to him by marrïage.
Love is a god, and marriage is but words;
And therefore *Mosby's* title is the best.
Tush! Whether it be or no, he shall be mine
In spite of him, of *Hymen,* and of rites.

Here enters Adam of the Flower-de-Luce

And here comes Adam of the *Flower-de-Luce.*
I hope he brings me tidings of my love.
How now, Adam, what is the news with you?
Be not afraid; my husband is now from home.

ADAM He whom you wot of, Mosby, Mistress Alice,
Is come to town, and sends you word by me
In any case you may not visit him.

ALICE Not visit him?

ADAM No, nor take no knowledge of his being here.

ALICE But tell me, is he angry or displeased?

ADAM Should seem so, for he is wondrous sad.

ALICE Were he as mad as raving Hercules,
I'll see him. Ay, and were thy house of force,
These hands of mine should raze it to the ground
Unless that thou wouldst bring me to my love.

ADAM Nay, an you be so impatient, I'll be gone.

1.101 **title** claim (to my heart). This word also resonates with notions of property and rank.
1.102 **Tush!** an expression of impatience
1.102 **it** i.e. Mosby's title
1.103 **him** Arden
1.103 **Hymen** the god of marriage
1.104 **Flower-de-Luce** (an inn in Faversham, a few minutes' walk from Arden's house)
1.108 **wot** know
1.114 **sad** serious
1.115 **raving Hercules** The narrator of Book 9 of Ovid's *Metamorphoses* tells of the centaur Nessus, who is shot by Hercules' arrow during an attempted rape of Deianira (Hercules' wife). Deianira gives Hercules a shirt soaked in the blood of Nessus believing that it will revive her husband's affections and fidelity. But Nessus' blood is poisonous and the shirt drives Hercules into suicidal madness.
1.116 **of force** fortified
1.119 **an** if

ALICE Stay, Adam, stay. Thou wert wont to be my friend.
Ask Mosby how I have incurred his wrath.
Bear him from me these pair of silver dice
With which we played for kisses many a time,
And when I lost I won, and so did he—
Such winning and such losing Jove send me!—
And bid him, if his love do not decline,
Come this morning but along my door
And as a stranger but salute me there.
This may he do without suspect or fear.

[*Then Adam takes the dice*]

ADAM I'll tell him what you say, and so farewell.

ALICE Do, and one day I'll make amends for all. *Exit Adam*
I know he loves me well but dares not come
Because my husband is so jealïous
And these my narrow-prying neighbour blabs
Hinder our meetings when we would confer.
But, if I live, that block shall be removed;
And, Mosby, thou that comes to me by stealth
Shalt neither fear the biting speech of men
Nor Arden's looks. As surely shall he die
As I abhor him and love only thee.

Here enters Michael

How now, Michael, whither are you going?

MICHAEL To fetch my master's nag. I hope you'll think on me.

ALICE Ay. But, Michael, see you keep your oath
And be as secret as you are resolute.

MICHAEL I'll see he shall not live above a week.

ALICE On that condition, Michael, here is my hand:
None shall have Mosby's sister but thyself.

MICHAEL I understand the painter here hard by

1.120 **wont** accustomed
1.121 **incurred** caused
1.125 **Jove** Jupiter, the chief Roman deity
1.134 **narrow-prying** excessively suspicious, nosy
1.134 **neighbour blabs** neighbourhood gossips and tattle-tales
1.136 **block** barrier
1.140 **abhor** loathe
1.142 **nag** horse
1.148 **hard by** nearby

Hath made report that he and *Sue* is sure.

ALICE There's no such matter, Michael; believe it not.

MICHAEL But he hath sent a dagger sticking in a heart,
With a verse or two stolen from a painted cloth,
The which I hear the wench keeps in her chest.
Well, let her keep it! I shall find a fellow
That can both write and read, and make rhyme too;
And, if I do well, I say no more.
I'll send from London such a taunting letter
As she shall eat the heart he sent with salt
And fling the dagger at the painter's head.

ALICE What needs all this? I say that Susan's thine.

MICHAEL Why, then I say that I will kill my master
Or anything that you will have me do.

ALICE But, Michael, see you do it cunningly.

MICHAEL Why, say I should be took, I'll ne'er confess
That you know anything; and Susan, being a maid,
May beg me from the gallows of the shrieve.

ALICE Trust not to that, Michael.

MICHAEL You cannot tell me: I have seen it, I.
But, mistress, tell her whether I live or die
I'll make her more worth than twenty painters can;
For I will rid mine elder brother away,
And then the farm of Boughton is mine own.
Who would not venture upon house and land
When he may have it for a right-down blow?

Here enters Mosby

1.149 **sure** betrothed
1.152 **painted cloth** An inexpensive alternative to woven tapestry, painted cloth was used for decorative purposes in households and as draperies in the theatre. They frequently incorporated images, verses, and mottoes.
1.153 **wench** young woman
1.153 **chest** heart; bodice
1.158 **As** that
1.158 **salt** tears
1.163 **cunningly** artfully
1.164 **took** captured
1.166 **beg...shrieve** (refers to the common belief that a virgin could save a condemned man by agreeing to take him as her husband)
1.166 **shrieve** sheriff
1.170 **worth** wealthy
1.171 **rid...away** i.e. kill him
1.172 **Boughton** (Boughton-under-Blean, a village in Kent)
1.174 **right-down blow** a powerful and direct attack (i.e. a blow that instantly brings him down)

ALICE Yonder comes Mosby. Michael, get thee gone,
And let not him nor any know thy drifts. *Exit Michael*
Mosby, my love!
MOSBY Away, I say, and talk not to me now.
ALICE A word or two, sweetheart, and then I will.
'Tis yet but early days: thou needst not fear.
MOSBY Where is your husband?
ALICE 'Tis now high water, and he is at the quay.
MOSBY There let him be. Henceforward know me not.
ALICE Is this the end of all thy solemn oaths?
Is this the fruit thy reconcilement buds?
Have I for this given thee so many favours,
Incurred my husband's hate, and (out alas!)
Made shipwreck of mine honour for thy sake?
And dost thou say, 'Henceforward know me not?'
Remember, when I locked thee in my closet,
What were thy words and mine? Did we not both
Decree to murder Arden in the night?
The heavens can witness, and the world can tell,
Before I saw that falsehood look of thine,
'Fore I was tangled with thy 'ticing speech,
Arden to me was dearer than my soul,
And shall be still. Base peasant, get thee gone,
And boast not of thy conquest over me,
Gotten by witchcraft and mere sorcery.
For what hast thou to countenance my love,
Being descended of a noble house
And matched already with a gentleman
Whose servant thou mayst be? And so farewell.
MOSBY Ungentle and unkind! Alice, now I see

1.176 **drifts** schemes
1.180 **early days** early in the day (i.e. too early to be caught)
1.182 **high water** high tide
1.185 **buds** develops, generates
1.186 **favours** expressions of love
1.190 **closet** private room
1.192 **Decree** agree
1.194 **falsehood** deceptive
1.195 **'Fore** before
1.195 **tangled** entangled
1.195 **'ticing** enticing
1.199 **mere** utter
1.200 **countenance** be in possession of
1.201 **Being** considering that I am

That which I ever feared and find too true:
A woman's love is as the lightning flame
Which even in bursting forth consumes itself.
To try thy constancy have I been strange.
Would I had never tried, but lived in hope!

ALICE What needs thou try me whom thou never found false?

MOSBY Yet pardon me for love is jealïous.

ALICE So lists the sailor to the mermaid's song;
So looks the traveller to the basilisk.
I am content for to be reconciled,
And that, I know, will be mine overthrow.

MOSBY Thine overthrow? First, let the world dissolve!

ALICE Nay, Mosby, let me still enjoy thy love;
And, happen what will, I am resolute.
My saving husband hoards up bags of gold
To make our children rich, and now is he
Gone to unload the goods that shall be thine,
And he and Franklin will to London straight.

MOSBY To London, Alice? If thou'lt be ruled by me,
We'll make him sure enough for coming there.

ALICE Ah, would we could!

MOSBY I happened on a painter yesternight,
The only cunning man of Christendom,
For he can temper poison with his oil
That whoso looks upon the work he draws

1.208 **strange** cold, distant

1.212 **lists** listens

1.212 **mermaid's song** (often associated with the mythological Siren's song, which was thought to entice sailors to annihilation at sea)

1.213 **basilisk** legendary serpent whose gaze was considered deadly

1.215 **that** jealousy

1.217 **still** always

1.219 **saving** frugal

1.220 **our children** Despite a reference to Alice and Arden's daughter in Holinshed, there are no children in the play. Alice seems to allude to either the children she will have with Mosby or her traditional role as a wife in a patriarchal society.

1.222 **straight** straightaway

1.224 **We'll...there** i.e. we will make him harmless enough by preventing him from going there. Mosby indicates that they should thwart Arden's trip to London in order to stop the 'unloading' of his *goods*.

1.227 **cunning** one who has magical knowledge

1.228 **temper** mix

1.229 **whoso** whosoever

Shall, with the beams that issue from his sight,
Suck venom to his breast and slay himself.
Sweet Alice, he shall draw thy counterfeit,
That Arden may, by gazing on it, perish.

ALICE Ay, but, Mosby, that is dangerous;
For thou or I, or any other else,
Coming into the chamber where it hangs, may die.

MOSBY Ay, but we'll have it covered with a cloth,
And hung up in the study for himself.

ALICE It may not be; for, when the picture's drawn,
Arden, I know, will come and show it me.

MOSBY Fear not. We'll have that shall serve the turn.
This is the painter's house; I'll call him forth.

ALICE But, Mosby, I'll have no such picture, I.

MOSBY I pray thee leave it to my discretion. How, Clarke!

Here enters Clarke

O, you are an honest man of your word; you served me well.

CLARKE Why, sir, I'll do it for you at any time,
Provided, as you have given your word,
I may have Susan Mosby to my wife.
For, as sharp-witted poets, whose sweet verse
Make heavenly gods break off their nectar draughts
And lay their ears down to the lowly earth,
Use humble promise to their sacred Muse,
So we that are the poets' favourites

1.230 **beams...sight** Following the works of Galen, sixteenth-century theories of sight stipulated that vision was the effect of vital spirits (*beams*) that emerged from the eyes through the act of looking. This was thought to activate the surrounding air, turning it into a material bridge between the viewer and object. In Galenic humoral theory, what was observed was thought to be absorbed materially into the human body.

1.232 **counterfeit** imitation, portrait

1.241 **have...turn** devise something that will deal with the situation

1.244 **Clarke** The painter is not named in Holinshed.

1.249 **sharp-witted** quick and inventive

1.250 **nectar** (the drink of the gods)

1.252 **Muse** In classical mythology, a Muse was one of the nine goddesses that presided over and inspired artistic creation.

1.253–4 **So...love** like poets, painters also need a Muse to inspire their creations

1.253 **poets' favourites** Alludes to Horace's *Ut pictura poesis*, which literally translates to 'as is painting, so is poetry'; it probably derived from *Poema pictura loquens, pictura poema silens* (Poetry is a speaking picture, painting is a silent poem), an apocryphal aphorism attributed to Simonides of Keos by Plutarch (originally in Greek). Both quotations were often used in the *paragone*, or the conventional rivalry between the sister arts.

Must have a love. Ay, love is the painter's Muse,
That makes him frame a speaking countenance,
A weeping eye that witnesses heart's grief.
Then tell me, Master Mosby, shall I have her?

ALICE 'Tis pity but he should; he'll use her well.

MOSBY Clarke, here's my hand; my sister shall be thine.

CLARKE Then, brother, to requite this courtesy
You shall command my life, my skill, and all.

ALICE Ah, that thou couldst be secret!

MOSBY Fear him not. Leave; I have talked sufficïent.

CLARKE [*to Alice*] You know not me that ask such questïons.
Let it suffice I know you love him well,
And fain would have your husband made away;
Wherein, trust me, you show a noble mind,
That rather than you'll live with him you hate
You'll venture life and die with him you love.
The like will I do for my Susan's sake.

ALICE Yet nothing could enforce me to the deed
But Mosby's love. [*To Mosby*] Might I without control
Enjoy thee still, then Arden should not die;
But, seeing I cannot, therefore let him die.

MOSBY Enough, sweet Alice; thy kind words makes me melt.
[*To Clarke*] Your trick of poisoned pictures we dislike.
Some other poison would do better far.

ALICE Ay, such as might be put into his broth,
And yet in taste not to be found at all.

CLARKE I know your mind, and here I have it for you.
Put but a dram of this into his drink,
Or any kind of broth that he shall eat,
And he shall die within an hour after.

[*Then he gives Alice the poison*]

ALICE As I am a gentlewoman, Clarke, next day

1.255 **frame** make, represent
1.255 **speaking countenance** a speaking subject
1.256 **A** and a
1.258 **but** unless
1.258 **use** treat; handle (in a sexual sense)
1.260 **requite** reciprocate
1.266 **fain** eagerly, willingly
1.272 **control** limitation
1.281 **dram** small amount

Thou and Susan shall be marrièd.
MOSBY And I'll make her dowry more than I'll talk of, Clarke.
CLARKE Yonder's your husband. Mosby, I'll be gone.

Here enter Arden and Franklin

ALICE In good time, see where my husband comes.
Master Mosby, ask him the question yourself. *Exit Clarke*
MOSBY Master Arden, being at London yesternight,
The Abbey lands whereof you are now possessed
Were offered me on some occasìon
By Greene, one of Sir Anthony Aucher's men.
I pray you, sir, tell me, are not the lands yours?
Hath any other interest herein?
ARDEN Mosby, that question we'll decide anon.
Alice, make ready my breakfast; I must hence. *Exit Alice*
As for the lands, Mosby, they are mine
By letters patents from his majesty.
But I must have a mandate for my wife:
They say you seek to rob me of her love.
Villain, what makes thou in her company?
She's no companion for so base a groom.
MOSBY Arden, I thought not on her; I came to thee.
But rather than I pocket up this wrong—
FRANKLIN What will you do, sir?
MOSBY Revenge it on the proudest of you both.

1.287 **Yonder's** there is
1.288 **In good time** at the appropriate moment
1.293 **Sir Anthony Aucher** a gentleman of Otterden, Kent. 'Aucher was one of the major purchasers of crown lands in Kent following the dissolution of the monasteries' (*ODNB*).
1.295 **any other** anyone else
1.295 **interest** legal right
1.296–303 **Mosby…groom** The shift in pronouns from *you* to *thou* in this speech signifies an adjustment of attitude and address. In sixteenth-century English, *you* is commonly used by inferiors when talking to superiors and *thou* is traditionally used by speakers as a marker of superiority or condescension. If used independently in dialogue, these class-specific pronouns are harmless and conventional. However, a shift from 'you' to 'thou' or 'thou' to 'you' in a speech usually signals a meaningful act of denigration.
1.296 **question** point at issue
1.296 **decide** resolve
1.296 **anon** presently
1.300 **mandate** an official order signifying ownership
1.303 **groom** servant
1.305 **pocket up this wrong** accept this accusation

Then Arden draws forth Mosby's sword

ARDEN So, sirrah, you may not wear a sword!
The statute makes against artìficers.
I warrant that I do. Now use your bodkin,
Your Spanish needle, and your pressing-iron,
For this shall go with me. And mark my words—
You, goodman botcher, 'tis to you I speak—
The next time that I take thee near my house,
Instead of legs I'll make thee crawl on stumps.

MOSBY Ah, Master Arden, you have injured me;
I do appeal to God and to the world.

FRANKLIN Why, canst thou deny thou wert a botcher once?

MOSBY Measure me what I am, not what I was.

ARDEN Why, what art thou now but a velvet drudge,
A cheating steward, and base-minded peasant?

MOSBY Arden, now thou hast belched and vomited
The rancorous venom of thy mis-swoll'n heart,
Hear me but speak: as I intend to live
With God and his elected saints in heaven,
I never meant more to solicit her;
And that she knows, and all the world shall see.
I loved her once (sweet Arden, pardon me);
I could not choose; her beauty fired my heart.
But time hath quenched these over-raging coals;

1.308–15 **So…stumps** The form of Arden's insults draw attention to his social superiority. Arden articulates Mosby's pursuit of Alice in terms of social (and not sexual) transgression.

1.308 **sirrah** (a commonplace address to inferiors that expresses contempt or rebuke)

1.308 **sword** (a phallic symbol of masculine, patriarchal (as well as social) authority)

1.309 **The statute** A statute passed under the reign of Edward III forbade anyone under the rank of gentleman from bearing arms.

1.309 **makes** stipulates

1.309 **artìficers** craftsmen, manual labourers (rather than gentlemen)

1.310 **I…do** I am legally authorized (to wear a sword)

1.310 **bodkin** a small piercing tool used for puncturing holes in cloth; dagger; small penis

1.311 **Spanish needle** used for embroidery

1.312 **this** Mosby's sword

1.313 **goodman** a form of address used to signify one beneath the rank of gentleman

1.316 **injured** insulted, reviled

1.320 **velvet drudge** menial servant dressed in expensive velvet clothes

1.323 **rancorous** bitter, resentful

1.323 **mis-swoll'n** exceptionally swollen

1.325 **elected** those chosen by God for salvation

And, Arden, though I now frequent thy house,
'Tis for my sister's sake, her waiting-maid,
And not for hers. Mayst thou enjoy her long!
Hell-fire and wrathful vengeance light on me
If I dishonour her or injure thee.

ARDEN Mosby, with these thy protestatïons
The deadly hatred of my heart is appeased,
And thou and I'll be friends if this prove true.
As for the base terms I gave thee late,
Forget them, Mosby. I had cause to speak
When all the knights and gentlemen of Kent
Make common table-talk of her and thee.

MOSBY Who lives that is not touched with slanderous tongues?

FRANKLIN Then, Mosby, to eschew the speech of men,
Upon whose general bruit all honour hangs,
Forbear his house.

ARDEN Forbear it? Nay, rather frequent it more.
The world shall see that I distrust her not.
To warn him on the sudden from my house
Were to confirm the rumour that is grown.

MOSBY By my faith, sir, you say true.
And therefore will I sojourn here awhile
Until our enemies have talked their fill;
And then, I hope, they'll cease, and at last confess
How causeless they have injured her and me.

ARDEN And I will lie at London all this term
To let them see how light I weigh their words.

Here enter Alice [*and Michael with a bowl of broth*]

ALICE Husband, sit down. Your breakfast will be cold.

ARDEN Come, Master Mosby, will you sit with us?

MOSBY I cannot eat, but I'll sit for company.

[*Then Arden, Franklin, and Mosby sit at the table*]

ARDEN Sirrah Michael, see our horse be ready. [*Exit Michael*]

1.331 **frequent** visit
1.339 **base terms** offences
1.344 **eschew** avoid
1.345 **bruit** opinion
1.346 **Forbear** keep clear of
1.352 **sojourn** remain
1.361 **horse** nominative plural of 'horses'

[*Then Arden starts to eat his broth, and pauses*]

ALICE Husband, why pause ye? Why eat you not?

ARDEN I am not well. There's something in this broth
That is not wholesome. Didst thou make it, Alice?

ALICE I did, and that's the cause it likes not you.

Then she throws down the broth on the ground

There's nothing that I do can please your taste.
You were best to say I would have poisoned you.
[*To Mosby*] I cannot speak or cast aside my eye,
But he imagines I have stepped awry.
[*To Arden*] Here's he that you cast in my teeth so oft;
Now will I be convinced or purge myself.
[*To Mosby*] I charge thee speak to this mistrustful man,
Thou that wouldst see me hang, thou, Mosby, thou.
What favour hast thou had more than a kiss
At coming or departing from the town?

MOSBY You wrong yourself and me to cast these doubts.
Your loving husband is not jealïous.

ARDEN Why, gentle Mistress Alice, cannot I be ill
But you'll accuse yourself?
Franklin, thou hast a box of mithridate;
I'll take a little to prevent the worst.

FRANKLIN Do so, and let us presently take horse.
My life for yours, ye shall do well enough.

ALICE Give me a spoon; I'll eat of it myself.
Would it were full of poison to the brim!
Then should my cares and troubles have an end.
Was ever silly woman so tormented?

ARDEN Be patient, sweet love: I mistrust not thee.

ALICE God will revenge it, Arden, if thou dost,

1.369 **stepped awry** become unfaithful
1.370 **he** Mosby
1.370 **cast in my teeth** shove in my face
1.371 **convinced** proven culpable (to Arden's suspicions)
1.371 **purge** clear, cleanse. Purging via phlebotomy (bloodletting), laxatives, and/or emetics were aggressive treatments for correcting humoral imbalances.
1.372 **mistrustful** distrustful
1.380 **mithridate** universal antidote
1.383 **ye...enough** everything will be satisfactory
1.387 **silly** foolish

For never woman loved her husband better
Than I do thee.

ARDEN I know it, sweet Alice. Cease to complain,
Lest that in tears I answer thee again.

[*Here enters Michael*]

FRANKLIN Come, leave this dallying, and let us away.

ALICE Forbear to wound me with that bitter word.
Arden shall go to London in my arms.

[*Then she embraces Arden*]

ARDEN Loath am I to depart, yet I must go.

ALICE Wilt thou to London then, and leave me here?
Ah, if thou love me, gentle Arden, stay.

[*Then Arden hesitates*]

Yet, if thy business be of great import,
Go if thou wilt; I'll bear it as I may.
But write from London to me every week,
Nay, every day, and stay no longer there
Than thou must needs, lest that I die for sorrow.

ARDEN I'll write unto thee every other tide.
And so farewell, sweet Alice, till we meet next.

ALICE Farewell, husband, seeing you'll have it so.
And Master *Franklin* , seeing you take him hence,
In hope you'll hasten him home I'll give you this.

And then she kisseth him

FRANKLIN An if he stay, the fault shall not be mine.
Mosby, farewell, and see you keep your oath.

MOSBY I hope he is not jealous of me now.

ARDEN No, Mosby, no. Hereafter think of me
As of your dearest friend, and so farewell.

Exeunt Arden, Franklin, and Michael

ALICE I am glad he is gone. He was about to stay,
But did you mark me then how I broke off?

MOSBY Ay, Alice, and it was cunningly performed.

I.394 **dallying** frivolous lingering
I.397 **Loath** hesitant; disinclined
I.405 **every other tide** every other hour
I.410 **An if** if
I.417 **cunningly** skilfully

But what a villain is this painter Clarke!
ALICE Was it not a goodly poison that he gave?
Why, he's as well now as he was before.
It should have been some fine confectïon
That might have given the broth some dainty taste.
This powder was too gross and palpable.
MOSBY But had he eaten but three spoonfuls more,
Then had he died, and our love continued.
ALICE Why, so it shall, Mosby, albeit he live.
MOSBY It is unpossible, for I have sworn
Never hereafter to solicit thee
Or—whilst he lives—once more impòrtune thee.
ALICE Thou shalt not need; I will importune thee.
What? Shall an oath make thee forsake my love?—
As if I have not sworn as much myself
And given my hand unto him in the church!
Tush, Mosby, oaths are words, and words is wind,
And wind is mutable. Then I conclude
'Tis childishness to stand upon an oath.
MOSBY Well provèd, Mistress Alice. Yet, by your leave,
I'll keep mine unbroken whilst he lives.
ALICE Ay, do, and spare not. His time is but short;
For, if thou be'st as resolute as I,
We'll have him murdered as he walks the streets.
In London many alehouse-ruffians keep,
Which, as I hear, will murder men for gold.
They shall be soundly fee'd to pay him home.

Here enters Greene

MOSBY Alice, what's he that comes yonder? Know'st thou him?
ALICE Mosby, begone; I hope 'tis one that comes

1.421 **confectïon** prepared compound; poison
1.423 **gross and palpable** crude and detectable
1.426 **albeit** although
1.427 **unpossible** impossible
1.429 **impòrtune** bother
1.434 **words is wind** (proverbial: 'Words are but wind' (Dent, W833))
1.435 **wind is mutable** (proverbial: 'As wavering as the wind' (Dent, W412))
1.435 **mutable** changeable
1.442 **ruffians** villains
1.442 **keep** stay, live
1.444 **soundly…home** paid well to murder him

To put in practice our intended drifts. *Exit Mosby*

GREENE Mistress Arden, you are well met.
I am sorry that your husband is from home
Whenas my purposed journey was to him.
Yet all my labour is not spent in vain,
For I suppose that you can full discourse
And flat resolve me of the thing I seek.

ALICE What is it, Master Greene? If that I may
Or can with safety, I will answer you.

GREENE I heard your husband hath the grant of late,
Confirmed by letters patents from the King,
Of all the lands of the Abbey of Faversham,
Generally entitled, so that all former grants
Are cut off, whereof I myself had one;
But now my interest by that is void.
This is all, Mistress Arden; is it true or no?

ALICE True, Master Greene: the lands are his in state,
And whatsoever leases were before
Are void for term of Master Arden's life.
He hath the grant under the Chancery seal.

GREENE Pardon me, Mistress Arden, I must speak,
For I am touched. Your husband doth me wrong
To wring me from the little land I have.
My living is my life; only that
Resteth remainder of my portïon.
Desire of wealth is endless in his mind,
And he is greedy-gaping still for gain;
Nor cares he, though young gentlemen do beg,
So he may scrape and hoard up in his pouch.

1.453 **flat resolve** make clear to
1.459 **Generally entitled** deeded without exceptions
1.459 **former grants** previous claims to the land
1.460 **cut off** supplanted
1.461 **interest** legal right to property
1.463 **in state** legally
1.466 **Chancery seal** official approval from the Court of the Lord Chancellor, the most powerful court in England next to the House of Lords
1.468 **touched** bothered
1.468 **doth** does
1.470 **living** property
1.471 **Resteth...portïon** i.e. is what remains of my inheritance
1.473 **greedy-gaping still** always excessively greedy
1.475 **So** so long as
1.475 **pouch** purse

But, seeing he hath taken my lands, I'll value life
As careless as he is careful for to get;
And tell him this from me: I'll be revenged,
And so as he shall wish the Abbey lands
Had rested still within their former state.

ALICE Alas, poor gentleman, I pity you,
And woe is me that any man should want.
God knows, 'tis not my fault! But wonder not
Though he be hard to others, when to me—
Ah, Master Greene, God knows how I am used!

GREENE Why, Mistress Arden, can the crabbèd churl
Use you unkindly? Respects he not your birth,
Your honourable friends, nor what you brought?
Why, all Kent knows your parentage and what you are.

ALICE Ah, Master Greene—be it spoken in secret here—
I never live good day with him alone.
When he is at home, then have I froward looks,
Hard words, and blows to mend the match withal.
And, though I might content as good a man,
Yet doth he keep in every corner trulls;
And when he's weary with his trugs at home,
Then rides he straight to London. There, forsooth,
He revels it among such filthy ones
As counsels him to make away his wife.
Thus live I daily in continual fear,
In sorrow, so despairing of redress
As every day I wish with hearty prayer
That he or I were taken forth the world.

1.477 **careful for to get** eager to acquire
1.479 **so as** in such a way
1.486–9 **Why...are** In contrast to Arden's linguistic gestures of self-identification with the gentry, Arden is framed here as socially inferior, acquisitive, and desirous of status.
1.486 **crabbèd** disagreeable
1.486 **churl** peasant
1.488 **what you brought** i.e. your substantial dowry
1.492 **froward** unpleasant
1.493 **mend the match withal** Alice ironically implies that Arden gives her *hard words* and *blows* to complement their union.
1.495 **trulls** prostitutes
1.496 **trugs** synonymous with *trulls*. In the seventeenth century, this word was also used to describe young boys that were in a sexual relationship with an older man.
1.501 **despairing of redress** distraught by the absence of help

GREENE Now trust me, Mistress Alice, it grieveth me
So fair a creature should be so abused.
Why, who would have thought the civil sir so sullen?
He looks so smoothly. Now fie upon him, churl!
An if he live a day, he lives too long.
But frolic, woman, I shall be the man
Shall set you free from all this discontent,
And if the churl deny my interest
And will not yield my lease into my hand,
I'll pay him home, whatever hap to me.

ALICE But speak you as you think?

GREENE Ay, God's my witness, I mean plain dealing,
For I had rather die than lose my land.

ALICE Then, Master Greene, be counsellèd by me:
Endanger not yourself for such a churl,
But hire some cutters for to cut him short;
And here's ten pound to wager them withal.

[*Then she gives Greene money*]

When he is dead you shall have twenty more—
And the lands whereof my husband is possessed
Shall be entitled as they were before.

GREENE Will you keep promise with me?

ALICE Or count me false and perjured whilst I live!

GREENE Then here's my hand: I'll have him so dispatched.

[*Then they shake hands*]

I'll up to London straight. I'll thither post
And never rest till I have compassed it.
Till then, farewell.

ALICE Good Fortune follow all your forward thoughts!—
And whosoever doth attempt the deed,
A happy hand I wish; and so farewell. [*Exit Greene*]
All this goes well. Mosby, I long for thee

1.507 **smoothly** well mannered
1.508 **An if** if
1.509 **frolic** cheer up
1.519 **cutters** cut-throats, assassins
1.520 **wager** hire
1.527 **thither post** travel to that place without delay
1.528 **compassed it** accomplished the task; reached London
1.530 **forward** fervent

To let thee know all that I have contrived.

Here enter Mosby and Clarke

MOSBY How now, Alice, what's the news?
ALICE Such as will content thee well, sweetheart.
MOSBY Well, let them pass awhile, and tell me, Alice,
How have you dealt and tempered with my sister?
What, will she have my neighbour Clarke, or no?
ALICE What, Master Mosby! Let him woo himself.
Think you that maids look not for fair words?
Go to her, Clarke; she's all alone within.
Michael, my man, is clean out of her books.
CLARKE I thank you, Mistress Arden. I will in;
And, if fair Susan and I can make a gree,
You shall command me to the uttermost
As far as either goods or life may stretch. *Exit Clarke*
MOSBY Now, Alice, let's hear thy news.
ALICE They be so good that I must laugh for joy
Before I can begin to tell my tale.
MOSBY Let's hear them, that I may laugh for company.
ALICE This morning Master Greene—Dick Greene, I mean,
From whom my husband had the Abbey land—
Came hither railing for to know the truth
Whether my husband had the lands by grant.
I told him all, whereat he stormed amain
And swore he would cry quittance with the churl
And, if he did deny his interest,
Stab him, whatsoever did befall himself.
Whenas I saw his choler thus to rise,
I whetted on the gentleman with words;

1.537 **them** i.e. the news

1.538 **tempered with** worked upon, influenced

1.543 **clean…books** i.e. out of her favour. The phrase is proverbial: 'To be in (out of) one's books' (Dent, B534).

1.545 **a gree** an agreement

1.554 **railing for** raving in order to

1.556 **whereat** at which, in response to which

1.556 **stormed amain** vehemently raged

1.557 **cry quittance** get even

1.560 **choler** anger, yellow bile. A person with a choleric disposition suffered from an excess of yellow bile (one of the four humours that was thought to determine an individual's psycho-physiological well-being).

1.561 **whetted on** provoked

And, to conclude, Mosby, at last we grew
To composition for my husband's death.
I gave him ten pound for to hire knaves,
By some device to make away the churl;
When he is dead, he should have twenty more
And repossess his former lands again.
On this we 'greed, and he is ridden straight
To London to bring his death about.

MOSBY But call you this good news?

ALICE Ay, sweetheart, be they not?

MOSBY 'Twere cheerful news to hear the churl were dead;
But trust me, Alice, I take it passing ill
You would be so forgetful of our state
To make recount of it to every groom.
What? To acquaint each stranger with our drifts,
Chiefly in case of murder? Why, 'tis the way
To make it open unto Arden's self,
And bring thyself and me to ruin both.
Forewarned, forearmed: who threats his enemy
Lends him a sword to guard himself withal.

ALICE I did it for the best.

MOSBY Well, seeing 'tis done, cheerily let it pass.
You know this Greene: is he not religious?
A man, I guess, of great devotïon.

ALICE He is.

MOSBY Then, sweet Alice, let it pass. I have a drift
Will quiet all, whatever is amiss.

Here enter Clarke and Susan

ALICE How now, Clarke? Have you found me false?
Did I not plead the matter hard for you?

CLARKE You did.

MOSBY And what? Will't be a match?

1.563 **composition** mutual agreement
1.572 **passing** very
1.576 **in case** on the subject
1.579 **Forewarned, forearmed** (proverbial (Dent, H54))
1.583 **religious** pious (and thus not a dependable accomplice to Arden's murder)

CLARKE A match, i'faith, sir. Ay, the day is mine.
The painter lays his colours to the life;
His pencil draws no shadows in his love;
Susan is mine.

ALICE You make her blush.

MOSBY What, sister, is it Clarke must be the man?

SUSAN It resteth in your grant. Some words are passed,
And haply we be grown unto a match,
If you be willing that it shall be so.

MOSBY Ah, Master Clarke, it resteth at my grant;
You see my sister's yet at my dispose;
But, so you'll grant me one thing I shall ask,
I am content my sister shall be yours.

CLARKE What is it, Master Mosby?

MOSBY I do remember once in secret talk,
You told me how you could compound by art
A crucifix empoisonèd,
That whoso look upon it should wax blind
And with the scent be stifled, that ere long
He should die poisoned that did view it well.
I would have you make me such a crucifix,
And then I'll grant my sister shall be yours.

CLARKE Though I am loath, because it toucheth life,
Yet, rather ere I'll leave sweet Susan's love,
I'll do it, and with all the haste I may.
But for whom is it?

ALICE Leave that to us. Why, Clarke, is it possible
That you should paint and draw it out yourself,
The colours being baleful and impoisonèd,

1.592–3 **the painter... love** Because the painter vividly imitates life in his paintings, there is no need to cast pallor on love (the subject of his painting) since he has possession of his beloved.

1.596 **grant** permission. Following the patriarchal imperatives of sixteenth-century England, Susan acquiesces to the authority of her brother in place of her father.

1.597 **haply** maybe

1.600 **dispose** subject to my power to arrange her affairs

1.606 **crucifix empoisonèd** poisoned crucifix

1.607 **wax blind** become blind

1.612 **loath** hesitant

1.613 **Yet... love** i.e. I'd rather do that than abandon Susan's love

1.618 **baleful** harmful

And no ways prejudice yourself withal?
MOSBY Well questioned, Alice. Clarke, how answer you that?
CLARKE Very easily. I'll tell you straight
How I do work of these impoisoned drugs:
I fasten on my spectacles so close
As nothing can any way offend my sight;
Then, as I put a leaf within my nose,
So put I rhubarb to avoid the smell,
And softly as another work I paint.
MOSBY 'Tis very well, but against when shall I have it?
CLARKE Within this ten days.
MOSBY 'Twill serve the turn.
Now, Alice, let's in and see what cheer you keep.
[Exit Clarke with Susan]
I hope, now Master Arden is from home,
You'll give me leave to play your husband's part.
ALICE Mosby, you know who's master of my heart,
He well may be the master of the house. *Exeunt*

Sc. 2

Here enter Greene and Bradshaw

BRADSHAW See you them that comes yonder, Master Greene?
GREENE Ay, very well. Do you know them?

Here enter Black Will and Shakebag

BRADSHAW The one I know not, but he seems a knave,
Chiefly for bearing the other company;
For such a slave, so vile a rogue as he,
Lives not again upon the earth.
Black Will is his name. I tell you, Master Greene,

1.619 **prejudice** expose
1.624 **offend** injure
1.626 **rhubarb** bitter plant often used for its medicinal properties as a purgative
1.627 **softly as another** as easily as anyone
1.632 **play...part** i.e. become her lover; a metatheatrical assertion of Arden's role in the play as a claimant of rank through the possession of the Abbey lands. Mosby insinuates that by owning Alice he will elevate his status (and thus *play* the *part* of an upwardly mobile social agent).
1.633 **who's** whoever is

Sc. 2 2.6 **again** elsewhere

At Boulogne he and I were fellow soldiers,
Where he played such pranks
As all the camp feared him for his villainy.
I warrant you he bears so bad a mind
That for a crown he'll murder any man.

[*Then Bradshaw makes to leave*]

GREENE [*aside*] The fitter is he for my purpose, marry.

WILL How now, fellow Bradshaw? Whither away so early?

BRADSHAW O Will, times are changed: no fellows now,
Though we were once together in the field;
Yet thy friend to do thee any good I can.

WILL Why, Bradshaw, was not thou and I fellow soldiers at Boulogne, where I was a corporal and thou but a base mercenary groom? 'No fellows now' because you are a goldsmith and have a little plate in your shop? You were glad to call me 'fellow Will' and, with a curtsy to the earth, 'One snatch, good corporal' when I stole the half ox from John the victualler and domineered with it amongst good fellows in one night.

BRADSHAW Ay, Will, those days are past with me.

WILL Ay, but they be not past with me—
for I keep that same honourable mind still. Good neighbour Bradshaw, you are too proud to be my fellow; but, were it not that I see more company coming down the hill, I would be fellows with you once more, and share crowns with you too. But let that pass, and tell me whither you go.

BRADSHAW To London, Will, about a piece of service
Wherein haply thou mayst pleasure me.

WILL What is it?

2.8 **Boulogne** (pronounced 'bùllen'). French seaport on the English Channel, captured by Henry VIII in 1544, but conceded back to the French by Edward VI in 1550.

2.11 **warrant** assure

2.12 **crown** a coin worth five shillings (or one quarter of a pound)

2.13 **marry** i.e. 'by the Virgin Mary' (an intensifier or interjection that had lost most of its original meaning)

2.16 **field** field of battle

2.19–20 **base mercenary groom** (a hired soldier, and thus inferior to an enlisted soldier)

2.22 **curtsy** bow

2.22 **snatch** small piece

2.23 **victualler** provider of food and drink

2.23 **domineered** dominated, rejoiced

2.30 **share crowns with you** i.e. rob you

BRADSHAW Of late Lord Cheyne lost some plate,
Which one did bring and sold it at my shop,
Saying he served Sir Anthony Cooke.
A search was made, the plate was found with me,
And I am bound to answer at the 'size.
Now Lord Cheyne solemnly vows, if law will serve him, he'll hang me for his plate. Now I am going to London upon hope to find the fellow. Now, Will, I know thou art acquainted with such companions.

WILL What manner of man was he?

BRADSHAW A lean-faced, writhen knave,
Hawk-nosed and very hollow-eyed,
With mighty furrows in his stormy brows,
Long hair down to his shoulders curled;
His chin was bare, but on his upper lip
A moustache, which he wound about his ear.

WILL What apparel had he?

BRADSHAW A watchet satin doublet all to-torn,
(The inner side did bear the greater show);
A pair of threadbare velvet hose, seam rent;
A worsted stocking rent above the shoe;
A livery cloak, but all the lace was off—
'Twas bad, but yet it served to hide the plate.

2.35 **Cheyne** (pronounced 'chay-nee'): Sir Thomas Cheyne (1485–1588), warden of the Cinque Ports and Kent's representative in Parliament

2.37 **Sir Anthony Cooke** Cooke (1504–76) was a prominent anti-Catholic politician and, in all likelihood, a tutor to Protestant King Edward VI. He was famous for his five exceptionally well-educated daughters, some still prominent and powerful Protestants in 1592: one married to Lord Burghley, another to the elder Francis Bacon, and the third (Elizabeth Russell) the active and formidable widow of the Earl of Bedford.

2.39 **'size** assize (legislative session)

2.43 **companions** i.e. knaves

2.44 **What...he** What did he look like?

2.45 **writhen** misshapen

2.47 **furrows** wrinkles

2.48 **Long hair** a signifier of lawlessness

2.52 **watchet** light blue

2.52 **doublet** close-fitting body garment, typical apparel for men

2.52 **to-torn** torn apart

2.53 **The inner...show** (the lining of the doublet was more visible than the external fabric)

2.54 **threadbare** worn out

2.54 **hose** leggings

2.54 **rent** torn

2.55 **worsted** woollen

WILL [*aside to Shakebag*] Sirrah Shakebag, canst thou remember since we trolled the bowl at Sittingbourne, where I broke the tapster's head of the Lion with a cudgel-stick?

SHAKEBAG [*aside to Will*] Ay, very well, Will.

WILL [*aside to Shakebag*] Why, it was with the money that the plate was sold for. [*Aloud*] Sirrah Bradshaw, what wilt thou give him that can tell thee who sold thy plate?

BRADSHAW Who, I pray thee, good Will?

WILL Why, 'twas one Jack Fitten. He's now in Newgate for stealing a horse, and shall be arraigned the next 'size.

BRADSHAW Why then, let Lord Cheyne seek Jack Fitten forth, for I'll back and tell him who robbed him of his plate. This cheers my heart. Master Greene, I'll leave you, for I must to the Isle of Sheppey with speed.

GREENE Before you go, let me entreat you to carry this letter to Mistress Arden of Faversham, and humbly recommend me to herself.

[*Then he gives Bradshaw a letter*]

BRADSHAW That will I, Master Greene, and so farewell.

[*Then he gives Will money*]

Here Will, there's a crown for thy good news.

WILL Farewell, Bradshaw. I'll drink no water for thy sake whilst this lasts. *Exit Bradshaw.*

Now, gentleman, shall we have your company to London?

GREENE Nay, stay, sirs.
A little more I needs must use your help,
And in a matter of great consequence—
Wherein, if you'll be secret and profound,

2.59 **trolled the bowl** revelled; passed around the drinking cup
2.59 **Sittingbourne** (a town in Kent roughly nine miles from Faversham, on the Pilgrims' Road to Canterbury)
2.60 **tapster's** innkeeper's
2.60 **the Lion** the Lion's Inn
2.60 **cudgel-stick** a club
2.66 **Newgate** London's principal prison
2.71 **Isle of Sheppey** (an island in Kent, on the south side of the Thames Estuary just opposite Faversham)
2.76 **drink no water** (because he would rather drink wine than water)
2.82 **profound** crafty

I'll give you twenty angels for your pains.

WILL How? Twenty angels? Give my fellow George Shakebag and me twenty angels, and, if thou'lt have thy own father slain that thou mayst inherit his land, we'll kill him.

SHAKEBAG Ay, thy mother, thy sister, thy brother, or all thy kin.

GREENE Well, this it is: Arden of Faversham
Hath highly wronged me about the Abbey land,
That no revenge but death will serve the turn.
Will you two kill him? Here's the angels down,
And I will lay the platform of his death.

WILL Plat me no platforms! Give me the money, and I'll stab him as he stands pissing against a wall, but I'll kill him.

SHAKEBAG Where is he?

GREENE He is now at London, in Aldersgate Street.

SHAKEBAG He's dead as if he had been condemned by an act of Parliament, if once Black Will and I swear his death.

GREENE Here is ten pound;

[*Then he gives them money*]

and, when he is dead, ye shall have twenty more.

WILL My fingers itches to be at the peasant. Ah, that I might be set awork thus through the year, and that murder would grow to an occupation, that a man might work without danger of law—'swounds, I warrant I should be warden of the company! Come, let us be going, and we'll bait at Rochester, where I'll give thee a gallon of sack to handsel the match withal. *Exeunt*

2.83 **angels** gold coins worth ten shillings (or half a pound)
2.90 **will serve the turn** will be suitable
2.92 **lay the platform** devise the plan for
2.93 **Plat** plot
2.96 **Aldersgate Street** Fashionable street that ran south from Aldersgate (one of the gates of the original walled medieval city of London) to the west end of Cheapside (an upscale shopping street).
2.104 **'swounds** (a curse, contracting the very blasphemous oath, 'By God's wounds')
2.104 **warden of the company** Black Will imagines himself as a governing member of a *company* of murderers arranged like one of the certified livery companies of the City of London.
2.105 **bait at Rochester** i.e. stop for food and drink at Rochester (a city in Kent between London and Faversham)
2.106 **sack** Spanish wine
2.106 **handsel** salute, confirm

Sc. 3

Here enters Michael [with a letter]

MICHAEL I have gotten such a letter as will touch the painter, and thus it is:

Here enter Arden and Franklin and hears Michael read this letter

'My duty remembered, Mistress Susan, hoping in God you be in good health, as I, Michael, was at the making hereof. This is to certify you that, as the turtle true, when she hath lost her mate, sitteth alone, so I, mourning for your absence, do walk up and down Paul's, till one day I fell asleep and lost my master's pantofles. Ah, Mistress Susan, abolish that paltry painter, cut him off by the shins with a frowning look of your crabbed countenance, and think upon Michael, who, drunk with the dregs of your favour, will cleave as fast to your love as a plaster of pitch to a galled horseback. Thus hoping you will let my passions penetrate, or rather impetrate mercy of your meek hands, I end.

Yours,
Michael, or else not *Michael*.'

ARDEN Why, you paltry knave,
Stand you here loitering, knowing my affairs,
What haste my business craves to send to Kent?

FRANKLIN 'Faith, friend Michael, this is very ill,
Knowing your master hath no more but you—
And do ye slack his business for your own?

ARDEN Where is the letter, sirrah? Let me see it.

Then [Michael] gives him the letter

See, Master Franklin, here's proper stuff:

Sc. 3 3.1 **touch** anger
3.5 **turtle** turtle dove, an emblem of constancy
3.7 **Paul's** (St Paul's Churchyard, the publishing and bookselling centre of London and a common gathering place for merchants, con-men, and crooks)
3.8 **pantofles** overshoes
3.9 **crabbed** irritable
3.10 **dregs** remains
3.11 **plaster of pitch** dressing steeped in balm or resin to treat diseased horses; can also hint at promiscuity
3.11 **galled** chafed
3.12 **let my passions penetrate** let my intentions or feelings for you become clear; let me engage in sexual intercourse
3.13 **impetrate** plead
3.13 **mercy** i.e. the mercy
3.16 **paltry** meagre, insignificant
3.18 **to send** i.e. to be sent

Susan my maid, the painter, and my man,
A crew of harlots, all in love, forsooth.
[*To Michael*] Sirrah, let me hear no more of this,
Nor, for thy life, once write to her a word.

Here enter Greene, Will, and Shakebag

Will thou be married to so base a trull?
'Tis Mosby's sister. Come I once at home,
I'll rouse her from remaining in my house.
Now, Master Franklin, let us go walk in Paul's.
Come, but a turn or two, and then away.

Exeunt [*Arden, Franklin, and Michael*]

GREENE The first is Arden, and that's his man;
The other is Franklin, Arden's dearest friend.

WILL 'Swounds, I'll kill them all three.

GREENE Nay, sirs, touch not his man in any case.
But stand close, and take your fittest standing,
And, at his coming forth, speed him.
But now I'll leave you till the deed be done.
To the Nag's Head; there's this coward's haunt. *Exit Greene*

SHAKEBAG If he be not paid his own, ne'er trust Shakebag.

WILL Sirrah Shakebag, at his coming forth I'll run him through, and then to the Blackfriars and there take water and away.

SHAKEBAG Why, that's the best; but see thou miss him not.

WILL How can I miss him, when I think on the forty angels I must have more?

Here enters a Prentice

PRENTICE 'Tis very late; I were best shut up my stall, for here will be old filching when the press comes forth of Paul's.

3.25 **harlots** lecherous persons
3.29 **Come...at** as soon as I come
3.30 **rouse** shake; force to emerge from safety (as in hunting); stir
3.36 **in any case** on any account
3.37 **stand close** hide
3.37 **fittest standing** optimal position (for the hunting of game)
3.38 **speed** kill
3.40 **Nag's Head** (tavern in London, at the east corner of Cheapside and Friday Street. See 'Aldersgate Street' above.)
3.41 **paid his own** i.e. murdered
3.43 **Blackfriars** (a gated exclusive district in London, near St Paul's Cathedral, with easy access to the river)
3.43 **take water** negotiate the Thames by boat
3.46.1 **Prentice** apprentice
3.47 **stall** wooden structure that displays goods for sale (i.e. book stall)
3.48 **old filching** abundant thieving
3.48 **press** crowd (leaving a sermon)

Then lets he down his window, and it breaks Black Will's head

WILL 'Swounds, draw, Shakebag, draw! I am almost killed.

[*Then Will and Shakebag draw their swords, and the press comes forth of Paul's*]

PRENTICE We'll tame you, I warrant.

WILL 'Swounds, I am tame enough already.

Here enter Arden, Franklin, and Michael

ARDEN What troublesome fray or mutiny is this?

FRANKLIN 'Tis nothing but some brabbling, paltry fray,
Devised to pick men's pockets in the throng.

ARDEN Is't nothing else? Come, Franklin, let us away.

Exeunt [*Arden, Franklin, and Michael*]

WILL What 'mends shall I have for my broken head?

PRENTICE Marry, this 'mends: that if you get you not away all the sooner, you shall be well beaten and sent to the Counter.

WILL Well, I'll be gone; but look to your signs, for I'll pull them down all. [*Exit prentice and the press*]
Shakebag, my broken head grieves me not so much as by this means Arden hath escaped.

Here enters Greene

I had a glimpse of him and his companion.

GREENE Why, sirs, Arden's as well as I. I met him and Franklin going merrily to the ordinary. What, dare you not do it?

WILL Yes, sir, we dare do it. But, were my consent to give again, we would not do it under ten pound more. I value every drop of my blood at a French crown. I have had ten pound to steal a dog, and we have no more here to kill a man. But that a bargain is a bargain and so forth, you should do it yourself.

GREENE I pray thee, how came thy head broke?

3.50 **tame** injure
3.52 **fray** skirmish
3.53 **brabbling** disorderly, loud
3.56 **'mends** treatment
3.58 **the Counter** (a prison in Southwark)
3.59 **signs** i.e. shop-signs
3.65 **ordinary** tavern or inn that served meals at a fixed price
3.68 **French crown** the French *écu*, worth just under five shillings; baldness associated with syphilis

WILL Why, thou seest it is broke, dost thou not?

SHAKEBAG Standing against a stall, watching Arden's coming, a boy let down his shop window and broke his head; whereupon arose a brawl, and in the tumult Arden escaped us and passed by unthought on. But forbearance is no acquittance: another time we'll do it, I warrant thee.

GREENE I pray thee, Will, make clean thy bloody brow,
And let us bethink us on some other place
Where Arden may be met with handsomely.
Remember how devoutly thou hast sworn
To kill the villain; think upon thine oath.

WILL Tush, I have broken five hundred oaths!
But wouldst thou charm me to effect this deed,
Tell me of gold, my resolution's fee;
Say thou seest Mosby kneeling at my feet,
Off'ring me service for my high attempt;
And sweet Alice Arden, with a lap of crowns,
Comes with a lowly curtsy to the earth,
Saying, 'Take this but for thy quarterage;
Such yearly tribute will I answer thee.'
Why, this would steel soft-mettled cowardice,
With which Black Will was never tainted with.
I tell thee, Greene, the forlorn traveller
Whose lips are glued with summer's parching heat
Ne'er longed so much to see a running brook
As I to finish Arden's tragedy.
Seest thou this gore that cleaveth to my face?
From hence ne'er will I wash this bloody stain
Till Arden's heart be panting in my hand.

GREENE Why, that's well said. But what saith Shakebag?

SHAKEBAG I cannot paint my valour out with words.
But give me place and opportunity,

3.76 **forbearance is no acquittance** (proverbial (Dent, F584))
3.88 **lap of crowns** dress filled with coins (with bawdy undertones)
3.90 **quarterage** quarterly payment
3.91 **answer** assure
3.92 **steel** harden
3.92 **soft-mettled** gentle, soft; with wordplay on metal (steel)
3.98 **gore** blood
3.103 **give me** if only given

Such mercy as the starven lioness,
When she is dry-sucked of her eager young,
Shows to the prey that next encounters her,
On Arden so much pity would I take.

GREENE So should it fare with men of firm resolve.
And now, sirs, seeing this accident
Of meeting him in Paul's hath no success,
Let us bethink us on some other place
Whose earth may swallow up this Arden's blood.

Here enters Michael

See, yonder comes his man. And wot you what?
The foolish knave is in love with Mosby's sister—
And for her sake, whose love he cannot get
Unless Mosby solicit his suit,
The villain hath sworn the slaughter of his master.
We'll question him, for he may stead us much.
How now, Michael, whither are you going?

MICHAEL My master hath new supped,
And I am going to prepare his chamber.

GREENE Where supped Master Arden?

MICHAEL At the Nag's Head, at the eighteen-pence ordinary.—
How now, Master Shakebag?—What, Black Will! God's dear lady, how chance your face is so bloody?

WILL Go to, sirrah! There is a chance in it.
This sauciness in you will make you be knocked.

MICHAEL Nay, an you be offended, I'll be gone.

GREENE Stay, Michael; you may not 'scape us so.
Michael, I know you love your master well.

MICHAEL Why, so I do. But wherefore urge you that?

GREENE Because I think you love your mistress better.

MICHAEL So think not I. But say, i'faith, what if I should?

SHAKEBAG Come to the purpose. Michael, we hear

3.104 **starven** starving
3.113 **wot** know
3.118 **stead us much** provide us with useful information
3.124–5 **God's dear lady** i.e. the Virgin Mary
3.126 **Go to** (an exclamation of disapproval)
3.127 **sauciness** impudence

You have a pretty love in Faversham.
MICHAEL Why, have I two or three, what's that to thee?
WILL You deal too mildly with the peasant.
[*To Michael*] Thus it is:
'Tis known to us you love Mosby's sister;
We know besides that you have ta'en your oath
To further Mosby to your mistress' bed
And kill your master for his sister's sake.
Now, sir, a poorer coward than yourself
Was never fostered in the coast of Kent.
How comes it then that such a knave as you
Dare swear a matter of such consequence?
GREENE Ah, Will—
WILL Tush, give me leave.—There's no more but this:
Sith thou hast sworn, we dare discover all;
And, hadst thou or shouldst thou utter it,
We have devised a complot underhand,
Whatever shall betide to any of us,
To send thee roundly to the devil of hell.
And therefore thus: I am the very man,
Marked in my birth-hour by the Destinies,
To give an end to Arden's life on earth;
Thou but a member but to whet the knife
Whose edge must search the closet of his breast.
Thy office is but to appoint the place
And train thy master to his tragedy;
Mine, to perform it when occasion serves.
Then be not nice, but here devise with us
How and what way we may conclude his death.

3.148 **Sith** Since
3.150–62 **complot...death** The procedural language here links the collaborative subtleties of Arden's murder to the collective energies required for the performance of a play.
3.150 **complot** plot, scheme; a plot (or plat) was also a document displayed in the theatre that recapitulated the action of the play scene by scene.
3.150 **underhand** in secret
3.151 **betide** happen
3.154 **the Destinies** i.e. the three Fates of classical mythology
3.159 **train** lead
3.159 **tragedy** i.e. death. Calls attention to the play's dramatic genre.
3.160 **perform it** accomplish the task; act it out
3.161 **nice** coy, diffident
3.162 **conclude** determine; end with

SHAKEBAG So shalt thou purchase Mosby for thy friend,
And by his friendship gain his sister's love.

GREENE So shall thy mistress be thy favourer,
And thou disburdened of the oath thou made.

MICHAEL Well, gentlemen, I cannot but confess,
Sith you have urged me so apparently,
That I have vowed my master Arden's death;
And he whose kindly love and liberal hand
Doth challenge nought but good deserts of me
I will deliver over to your hands.
This night come to his house at Aldersgate.
The doors I'll leave unlocked against you come.
No sooner shall ye enter through the latch,
Over the threshold to the inner court,
But on your left hand shall you see the stairs
That leads directly to my master's chamber.
There take him and dispose him as ye please.
Now it were good we parted company.
What I have promisèd I will perform.

WILL Should you deceive us, 'twould go wrong with you.

MICHAEL I will accomplish all I have revealed.

WILL Come, let's go drink. Choler makes me as dry as a dog.

Exeunt Will, Greene, and Shakebag. Manet Michael

MICHAEL Thus feeds the lamb securely on the down
Whilst through the thicket of an arbour brake
The hunger-bitten wolf o'erpries his haunt
And takes advantage to eat him up.
Ah, harmless Arden, how, how hast thou misdone
That thus thy gentle life is levelled at?
The many good turns that thou hast done to me
Now must I quittance with betraying thee.

3.168 **apparently** plainly, completely
3.171 **nought** nothing
3.171 **deserts** deeds
3.174 **against you come** in preparation for your arrival
3.184.1 **Manet** he remains (Latin)
3.185 **down** hill
3.186 **thicket...brake** a grassy plot of land thick with vegetation
3.187 **o'erpries** spies on, watches over
3.187 **haunt** much frequented location
3.190 **levelled at** threatened
3.191 **turns** deeds
3.192 **quittance** repay

I, that should take the weapon in my hand
And buckler thee from ill-intending foes,
Do lead thee with a wicked, fraudful smile,
As unsuspected, to the slaughterhouse.
So have I sworn to Mosby and my mistress;
So have I promised to the slaughtermen;
And, should I not deal currently with them,
Their lawless rage would take revenge on me.
Tush, I will spurn at mercy for this once.
Let pity lodge where feeble women lie;
I am resolved, and Arden needs must die. *Exit Michael*

Sc. 4

Here enter Arden and Franklin

ARDEN No, Franklin, no. If fear or stormy threats,
If love of me or care of womanhood,
If fear of God or common speech of men
(Who mangle credit with their wounding words
And couch dishonour as dishonour buds)
Might 'join repentance in her wanton thoughts,
No question then but she would turn the leaf,
And sorrow for her dissolutïon.
But she is rooted in her wickedness,
Perverse and stubborn, not to be reclaimed.
Good counsel is to her as rain to weeds,
And reprehension makes her vice to grow
As *Hydra's* head that flourished by decay.
Her faults, methink, are painted in my face
For every searching eye to over-read;

3.194 **buckler** guard
3.196 **As unsuspected** I, being unsuspected
3.199 **currently** honourably

Sc. 4 4.4 **credit** reputation
4.5 **couch** plant in the earth; position
4.5 **buds** grows, germinates
4.6 **'join** enjoin
4.6 **in** of
4.6 **wanton** undisciplined
4.7 **turn the leaf** turn the page, start anew
4.8 **dissolutïon** immoral behaviour
4.12 **reprehension** censure
4.13 **Hydra's head** In Greek mythology, the many-headed Hydra was thought to regenerate two new heads for every one that was cut off.
4.13 **decay** destruction
4.15 **over-read** read

And Mosby's name, a scandal unto mine,
Is deeply trenchèd in my blushing brow.
Ah, Franklin, Franklin, when I think on this,
My heart's grief rends my other powers
Worse than the conflict at the hour of death.

FRANKLIN Gentle Arden, leave this sad lament.
She will amend, and so your griefs will cease;
Or else she'll die, and so your sorrows end.
If neither of these two do haply fall,
Yet let your comfort be that others bear
Your woes twice doubled, all with patïence.

ARDEN My house is irksome; there I cannot rest.

FRANKLIN Then stay with me in London; go not home.

ARDEN Then that base Mosby doth usurp my room
And makes his triumph of my being thence.
At home or not at home, where'er I be,
Here, here it lies, ah, Franklin, here it lies
That will not out till wretched Arden dies.

Here enters Michael

FRANKLIN Forget your griefs awhile. Here comes your man.

ARDEN What o'clock is't, sirrah?

MICHAEL Almost ten.

ARDEN See, see, how runs away the weary time!
Come, Master Franklin, shall we go to bed?

FRANKLIN I pray you, go before; I'll follow you.

Exeunt Arden and Michael. Manet Franklin

Ah, what a hell is fretful jealousy!
What pity-moving words, what deep-fetched sighs,
What grievous groans and overlading woes
Accompanies this gentle gentleman!

4.17 **trenchèd** carved
4.19 **rends** tears
4.24 **fall** befall, occur
4.27 **irksome** troubled
4.29 **usurp my room** take my place (in Alice's bed)
4.30 **thence** absent
4.40 **pity-moving words** words that move one to pity
4.40 **deep-fetched sighs** sighs fraught with deep despair
4.41 **overlading** weighty, substantial

Now will he shake his care-oppressèd head,
Then fix his sad eyes on the sullen earth,
Ashamed to gaze upon the open world;
Now will he cast his eyes up towards the heavens,
Looking that ways for redress of wrong.
Sometimes he seeketh to beguile his grief
And tells a story with his careful tongue;
Then comes his wife's dishonour in his thoughts
And in the middle cutteth off his tale,
Pouring fresh sorrow on his weary limbs.
So woe-begone, so inly charged with woe,
Was never any lived and bore it so.

Here enters Michael

MICHAEL My master would desire you come to bed.

FRANKLIN Is he himself already in his bed?

MICHAEL He is, and fain would have the light away.

Exit Franklin. Manet Michael

Conflicting thoughts encampèd in my breast
Awake me with the echo of their strokes,
And I, a judge to censure either side,
Can give to neither wishèd victory.
My master's kindness pleads to me for life
With just demand, and I must grant it him.
My mistress she hath forced me with an oath
For Susan's sake, the which I may not break,
For that is nearer than a master's love.
That grim-faced fellow, pitiless Black Will,
And Shakebag, stern in bloody stratagem
(Two rougher ruffians never lived in Kent),
Have sworn my death if I infringe my vow,
A dreadful thing to be considered of.
Methinks I see them with their boltered hair,
Staring and grinning in thy gentle face,

4.43–5 **shake...world** These are behavioural characteristics that associate Arden with a melancholic temperament (or an excess of black bile).

4.48 **beguile** deceive

4.57 **fain** willingly

4.59 **their** i.e. *conflicting thoughts*

4.60 **censure** evaluate

4.70 **infringe** break

4.72 **boltered** matted (with blood)

And in their ruthless hands their daggers drawn,
Insulting o'er thee with a peck of oaths,
Whilst thou, submissive, pleading for relief,
Art mangled by their ireful instruments.
Methinks I hear them ask where Michael is,
And pitiless Black Will cries, 'Stab the slave!
The peasant will detect the tragedy.'
The wrinkles in his foul, death-threat'ning face
Gapes open wide, like graves to swallow men.
My death to him is but a merriment,
And he will murder me to make him sport.
He comes, he comes! Ah, Master Franklin, help!
Call up the neighbours, or we are but dead!

Here enter Franklin and Arden

FRANKLIN What dismal outcry calls me from my rest?

ARDEN What hath occasioned such a fearful cry?
Speak, Michael! Hath any injured thee?

MICHAEL Nothing, sir; but, as I fell asleep
Upon the threshold, leaning to the stairs,
I had a fearful dream that troubled me,
And in my slumber thought I was beset
With murderer thieves that came to rifle me.
My trembling joints witness my inward fear.
I crave your pardons for disturbing you.

ARDEN So great a cry for nothing I ne'er heard.
What, are the doors fast locked and all things safe?

MICHAEL I cannot tell; I think I locked the doors.

ARDEN I like not this, but I'll go see myself.

[*Then he tries the doors*]

Ne'er trust me but the doors were all unlocked.
This negligence not half contenteth me.
Get you to bed; and, if you love my favour,

4.75 **Insulting** triumphing
4.75 **peck** heap
4.77 **ireful** hateful
4.80 **detect** expose
4.87 **dismal** cheerless
4.93–4 **beset with** attacked by
4.94 **murderer** murdering
4.94 **rifle** rob

Let me have no more such pranks as these.—
Come, Master Franklin, let us go to bed.
FRANKLIN Ay, by my faith; the air is very cold.
Michael, farewell. I pray thee dream no more. *Exeunt*

Sc. 5

Here enter Will, Greene, and Shakebag

SHAKEBAG Black night hath hid the pleasures of the day,
And sheeting darkness overhangs the earth
And with the black fold of her cloudy robe
Obscures us from the eyesight of the world;
In which sweet silence such as we triùmph.
The lazy minutes linger on their time,
Loath to give due audit to the hour,
Till in the watch our purpose be complete
And Arden sent to everlasting night.
Greene, get you gone, and linger hereabout,
And at some hour hence come to us again,
Where we will give you instance of his death.
GREENE Speed to my wish, whose will soe'er says no;
And so I'll leave you for an hour or two. *Exit Greene*
WILL I tell thee, Shakebag, would this thing were done!
I am so heavy that I can scarce go.
This drowsiness in me bodes little good.
SHAKEBAG How now, Will, become a precisïan?
Nay then, let's go sleep when bugs and fears
Shall kill our courages with their fancy's work.
WILL Why, Shakebag, thou mistakes me much

Sc. 5 5.2 **sheeting** covering, concealing
5.5 **such as we** i.e. murderers
5.7 **Loath** hesitant
5.7 **due audit to** rendering of accounts (with connotations of the Last Judgement); give an accurate report of
5.8 **watch** (each of the (three, four, or five) periods into which the night was divided . . . used rhetorically for the night-time; the state of being awake while others are asleep)
5.12 **instance** verification
5.13 **Speed** success
5.13 **whose** despite those whose
5.16 **heavy** gloomy, oppressed
5.16 **go** walk
5.18 **precisïan** puritan
5.19 **bugs** i.e. bugbears, invented horrors

And wrongs me too in telling me of fear.
Were't not a serious thing we go about,
It should be slipped till I had fought with thee
To let thee know I am no coward, I.
I tell thee, Shakebag, thou abusest me.

SHAKEBAG Why, thy speech bewrayed an inly kind of fear
And savoured of a weak, relenting spirit.
Go forward now in that we have begun,
And afterwards attempt me when thou darest.

WILL And if I do not, heaven cut me off!
But let that pass, and show me to this house,
Where thou shalt see I'll do as much as Shakebag.

SHAKEBAG This is the door.

[*He tries to open the door*]

But soft, methinks 'tis shut.
The villain Michael hath deceivèd us.

WILL Soft, let me see.

[*He tries to open the door*]

Shakebag, 'tis shut indeed.
Knock with thy sword: perhaps the slave will hear.

[*Shakebag knocks on the door with the handle of his sword*]

SHAKEBAG It will not be: the white-livered peasant
Is gone to bed and laughs us both to scorn.

WILL And he shall buy his merriment as dear
As ever coistrel bought so little sport.
Ne'er let this sword assist me when I need,
But rust and canker after I have sworn,
If I, the next time that I meet the hind,
Lop not away his leg, his arm, or both.

SHAKEBAG And let me never draw a sword again,

5.22 **telling** accusing
5.24 **slipped** disregarded
5.27 **bewrayed** revealed
5.28 **savoured of** tasted of, indicated
5.28 **relenting** lenient
5.30 **attempt** challenge
5.38 **white-livered** cowardly (as a result of a shortage of bile in the liver)
5.41 **coistrel** knave
5.43 **canker** i.e. decay
5.44 **hind** servant
5.45 **Lop** chop

Nor prosper in the twilight, cock-shut light,
When I would fleece the wealthy passenger,
But lie and languish in a loathsome den,
Hated and spit at by the goers-by,
And in that death may die, unpitièd,
If I, the next time that I meet the slave,
Cut not the nose from off the coward's face
And trample on it for this villainy.

WILL Come, let's go seek out Greene. I know he'll swear.

SHAKEBAG He were a villain an he would not swear.
'Twould make a pedant swear amongst his boys,
That ne'er durst say before but 'yea' and 'no',
To be thus flouted of a coistërel.

WILL Shakebag, let's seek out Greene, and in the morning
At the alehouse 'butting Arden's house
Watch the outcoming of that prick-eared cur,
And then let me alone to handle him. *Exeunt*

Sc. 6

Here enter Arden, Franklin, and Michael

ARDEN [*to Michael*] Sirrah, get you back to Billingsgate
And learn what time the tide will serve our turn.
Come to us in Paul's. First go make the bed,
And afterwards go hearken for the flood. *Exit Michael*
Come, Master Franklin, you shall go with me.
This night I dreamed that, being in a park,
A toil was pitched to overthrow the deer,
And I upon a little rising hill
Stood whistly watching for the herd's approach.
Even there methoughts a gentle slumber took me

5.47 **cock-shut light** 'a time of the evening at which poultry go to roost' (Samuel Johnson)
5.48 **passenger** traveller
5.58 **durst** does
5.59 **flouted** contemptuous
5.59 **coistërel** See note to 5.41.
5.61 **'butting** adjoining
5.62 **prick-eared** pointy-eared

Sc. 6 6.1 **Billingsgate** One of the gates of the City of London. The Billingsgate wharf was a popular point of arrival for travellers on the Thames.
6.4 **hearken** lie in wait
6.7 **toil** net
6.7 **pitched** spread
6.9 **whistly** quietly

And summoned all my parts to sweet repose;
But in the pleasure of this golden rest
An ill-thewed for'ster had removed the toil
And rounded me with that beguiling snare
Which late, methought, was pitched to cast the deer.
With that he blew an evil-sounding horn,
And at the noise another herdman came
With falchion drawn, and bent it at my breast,
Crying aloud, 'Thou art the game we seek.'
With this I waked, and trembled every joint
Like one obscurèd in a little bush
That sees a lion foraging about,
And, when the dreadful forest king is gone,
He pries about with timorous suspèct
Throughout the thorny casements of the brake,
And will not think his person dangerless,
But quakes and shivers, though the cause be gone.
So, trust me, Franklin, when I did awake,
I stood in doubt whether I waked or no,
Such great impression took this fond surprise.
God grant this vision bedeem me any good!

FRANKLIN This fantasy doth rise from Michael's fear,
Who being awakèd with the noise he made,
His troubled senses yet could take no rest;
And this, I warrant you, procured your dream.

ARDEN It may be so. God frame it to the best!
But oftentimes my dreams presage too true.

FRANKLIN To such as note their nightly fantasies,
Some one in twenty may incur belief.
But use it not; 'tis but a mockery.

ARDEN Come, Master Franklin, we'll now walk in Paul's,

6.13 **ill-thewed for'ster** wicked forester
6.14 **rounded...snare** i.e. trapped me in the net
6.18 **falchion** a sword (specifically, one that is curved and with an edge on the rounded side)
6.18 **bent** pointed
6.24 **suspèct** uncertainty
6.25 **casements** coverings
6.25 **brake** thicket
6.30 **fond surprise** foolish shock (caused by the dream)
6.31 **bedeem me any good** prophesies no threat to my life
6.36 **frame it** bring it about

And dine together at the ordinary,
And by my man's direction draw to the quay,
And with the tide go down to Faversham.
Say, Master Franklin, shall it not be so?

FRANKLIN At your good pleasure, sir; I'll bear you company.

Exeunt

Sc. 7

Here enters Michael at one door. Here enter Greene, Will, and Shakebag at another door

WILL Draw, Shakebag, for here's that villain Michael.

GREENE First, Will, let's hear what he can say.

WILL Speak, milksop slave, and never after speak!

MICHAEL For God's sake, sirs, let me excuse myself,
For here I swear, by heaven and earth and all,
I did perform the utmost of my task
And left the doors unbolted and unlocked.
But see the chance: Franklin and my master
Were very late conferring in the porch,
And Franklin left his napkin where he sat,
With certain gold knit in it, as he said.
Being in bed, he did bethink himself,
And coming down he found the doors unshut.
He locked the gates and brought away the keys;
For which offence my master rated me.
But now I am going to see what flood it is,
For with the tide my master will away,
Where you may front him well on Rainham Down,
A place well fitting such a stratagem.

WILL Your excuse hath somewhat mollified my choler.
Why now, Greene, 'tis better now nor e'er it was.

Sc. 7 7.3 **milksop** spineless
7.10 **napkin** handkerchief
7.11 **knit** gathered, tied up
7.15 **rated** berated, reprimanded
7.16 **flood** flood-tide
7.18 **front** confront
7.18 **Rainham Down** (countryside circumscribing Rainham, a village in Kent, on the Pilgrims' Road to Canterbury)
7.20 **mollified** soothed, balanced
7.21 **'tis…nor** it's no worse now than

GREENE But, Michael, is this true?

MICHAEL As true as I report it to be true.

SHAKEBAG Then, Michael, this shall be your penance: to feast us all at the Salutation, where we will plot our purpose throughly.

GREENE And, Michael, you shall bear no news of this tide, because they two may be in Rainham Down before your master.

MICHAEL Why, I'll agree to anything you'll have me, so you will accept of my company. *Exeunt*

Sc. 8

Here enters Mosby

MOSBY Disturbèd thoughts drives me from company
And dries my marrow with their watchfulness.
Continual trouble of my moody brain
Feebles my body by excess of drink,
And nips me as the bitter northeast wind
Doth check the tender blossoms in the spring.
Well fares the man, howe'er his cates do taste,
That tables not with foul suspicïon;
And he but pines amongst his delicates
Whose troubled mind is stuffed with discontent.
My golden time was when I had no gold.
Though then I wanted, yet I slept secure.
My daily toil begat me night's repose;
My night's repose made daylight fresh to me.
But, since I climbed the top bough of the tree
And sought to build my nest among the clouds,
Each gentlest airy gale doth shake my bed
And makes me dread my downfall to the earth.
But whither doth contemplation carry me?
The way I seek to find, where pleasure dwells,

7.25 **the Salutation** an inn and pub in Billingsgate
7.25 **throughly** thoroughly

Sc. 8 8.2 **marrow** essential substance; semen
8.4 **of drink** i.e. of drinking my thoughts
8.6 **check** arrest, impede
8.7 **cates** delicacies
8.8 **tables** dines
8.9 **pines** aches
8.13 **begat** procured
8.17 **gale** breeze (not modern 'storm')
8.17 **bed** i.e. *nest*

Is hedged behind me, that I cannot back
But needs must on, although to danger's gate.
Then, Arden, perish thou by that decree,
For Greene doth ear the land and weed thee up
To make my harvest nothing but pure corn.
And for his pains I'll hive him up awhile
And, after, smother him to have his wax;
Such bees as Greene must never live to sting.
Then is there Michael and the painter too,
Chief actors unto Arden's overthrow,
Who, when they shall see me sit in Arden's seat,
They will insult upon me for my meed
Or fright me by detecting of his end.
I'll none of that, for I can cast a bone
To make these curs pluck out each other's throat;
And then am I sole ruler of mine own.
Yet Mistress Arden lives. But she's myself,
An holy church rites makes us two but one.
But what for that? I may not trust you, Alice.
You have supplanted Arden for my sake
And will extirpen me to plant another.
'Tis fearful sleeping in a serpent's bed,
And I will cleanly rid my hands of her.

Here enters Alice [*with a prayer book in a gold binding*]

But here she comes, and I must flatter her.—
How now, Alice! What, sad and passionate?
Make me partaker of thy pensiveness.
Fire divided burns with lesser force.

8.21 **hedged** enclosed; obstructed
8.24 **ear** plough
8.24 **thee** i.e. Arden
8.25 **pure corn** i.e. untainted advantage
8.26 **hive** shelter him, keep him in a sweet place
8.27 **smother . . . wax** Bees were smoked out of their hives in order for beekeepers to reach their honey and wax.
8.32 **meed** prize
8.33 **detecting of** revealing, exposing
8.34 **cast a bone** (proverbial: 'He has cast a bone between them' (Dent, B518))
8.34 **bone** i.e. Susan
8.35 **these curs** i.e. Michael and the Painter
8.38 **holy church rites** marriage
8.41 **extirpen** root up, eradicate (another horticultural word)
8.43 **cleanly** skilfully
8.45 **passionate** full of emotion
8.47 **Fire** i.e. burning passion, love

ALICE But I will dam that fire in my breast
Till by the force thereof my heart consume. Ah, Mosby!

MOSBY Such deep pathaires, like to a cannon's burst
Discharged against a ruinated wall,
Breaks my relenting heart in thousand pieces.
Ungentle Alice, thy sorrow is my sore;
Thou know'st it well, and 'tis thy policy
To forge distressful looks to wound a breast
Where lies a heart that dies when thou art sad.
It is not love that loves to anger love.

ALICE It is not love that loves to murder love.

MOSBY How mean you that?

ALICE Thou know'st how dearly Arden lovèd me.

MOSBY And then?

ALICE And then—conceal the rest, for 'tis too bad,
Lest that my words be carried with the wind
And published in the world, to both our shames.
I pray thee, Mosby, let our springtime wither;
Our harvest else will yield but loathsome weeds.
Forget, I pray thee, what hath passed betwixt us,
For now I blush and tremble at the thoughts.

MOSBY What, are you changed?

ALICE Ay, to my former happy life again,
From title of an odious strumpet's name
To 'honest Arden's wife'. Not 'Arden's honest wife':
Ha, Mosby, 'tis thou hast rifled me of that,
And made me slanderous to all my kin.
Even in my forehead is thy name engraven,
A mean artìficer, that low-born name.
I was bewitched. Woe worth the hapless hour

8.48–9 **But...consume** I will confine that intense passion in my heart until it destroys itself.
8.48 **fire** (pronounced with two syllables)
8.50 **pathaires** passionate outbursts
8.51 **ruinated** predictively ruined
8.52 **relenting** yielding
8.55 **forge** design
8.64 **published** revealed
8.71 **odious** loathsome
8.71 **strumpet's** whore's
8.72 **honest wife** chaste wife
8.73 **rifled** robbed
8.76 **mean artìficer** lower-class manual labourer, low trickster
8.77 **Woe worth** a curse upon

And all the causes that enchanted me!
MOSBY Nay, if thou ban, let me breathe curses forth;
And, if you stand so nicely at your fame,
Let me repent the credit I have lost.
I have neglected matters of import
That would have stated me above thy state,
Forslowed advantages, and spurned at time.
Ay, Fortune's right hand Mosby hath forsook
To take a wanton giglot by the left.
I left the marriage of an honest maid
Whose dowry would have weighed down all thy wealth,
Whose beauty and demeanour far exceeded thee.
This certain good I lost for changing bad,
And wrapped my credit in thy company.
I 'was bewitched' (that is no theme of thine!)
And thou unhallowed hast enchanted me.
But I will break thy spells and exorcisms
And put another sight upon these eyes
That showed my heart a raven for a dove.
Thou art not fair: I viewed thee not till now.
Thou art not kind: till now I knew thee not.
And now the rain hath beaten off thy gilt,
Thy worthless copper shows thee counterfeit.
It grieves me not to see how foul thou art,
But mads me that I ever thought thee fair.
Go, get thee gone, a copesmate for thy hinds!
I am too good to be thy favourite.
ALICE Ay, now I see, and too soon find it true,
Which often hath been told me by my friends:
That Mosby loves me not but for my wealth—

8.79 **ban** curse
8.80 **stand...fame** obsess over your reputation
8.83 **stated...state** placed me above your social status
8.84 **Forslowed** squandered
8.85 **Fortune** (often personified as a goddess)
8.86 **giglot** lascivious woman
8.90 **changing** becoming
8.93 **unhallowed** profane
8.94 **exorcisms** conjurings; performances
8.96 **for** instead of
8.99 **gilt** thin layer of gold
8.100 **worthless...counterfeit** Counterfeit coins were usually made of base metals (like *copper*) plated with gold or silver.
8.103 **copesmate** companion
8.103 **hinds** servants (but also female deer)

Which, too incredulous, I ne'er believed.
Nay, hear me speak, Mosby, a word or two;
I'll bite my tongue if it speak bitterly.
Look on me, Mosby, or I'll kill myself;
Nothing shall hide me from thy stormy look.
If thou cry war, there is no peace for me.
I will do penance for offending thee
And burn this prayer book, where I here use
The holy word that had converted me.
See, Mosby, I will tear away the leaves,

[*Then she tears leaves from the prayer book*]

And all the leaves, and in this golden cover,
Shall thy sweet phrases and thy letters dwell,
And thereon will I chiefly meditate,
And hold no other faith but such devotion.
Wilt thou not look? Is all thy love overwhelmed?
Wilt thou not hear? What malice stops thine ears?
Why speaks thou not? What silence ties thy tongue?
Thou hast been sighted as the eagle is,
And heard as quickly as the fearful hare,
And spoke as smoothly as an orator,
When I have bid thee hear or see or speak;
And art thou sensible in none of these?
Weigh all thy good turns with this little fault,
And I deserve not Mosby's muddy looks.
A fount once troubled is not thickened still.
Be clear again, I'll ne'er more trouble thee.

MOSBY O, no, I am 'a base artìficer'.
My wings are feathered for a lowly flight.
Mosby? Fie, no! Not for a thousand pound.

8.112 **stormy** angry
8.115 **where** wherein
8.116 **converted me** i.e. made me chaste
8.121 **faith** religion (but playing on the sense of 'sexual and romantic fidelity')
8.121 **such devotion** i.e. Mosby's love
8.126 **And heard** and thou hast heard
8.126 **quickly** astutely
8.126 **fearful hare** (proverbial: 'As fearful as a hare' (Dent, H147))
8.127 **And spoke** and thou hast spoke
8.129 **sensible** able to feel
8.130 **thy good turns** i.e. your preferment
8.131 **muddy** troubled; melancholic
8.132 **A fount...still** a spring or fountain that is once clouded by stirred-up mud does not remain permanently polluted
8.135 **feathered...flight** (unlike Icarus, an emblem of ambition)

Make love to you? Why 'tis unpardonable.
We beggars must not breathe where gentles are.

ALICE Sweet Mosby is as gentle as a king,
And I too blind to judge him otherwise.
Flowers do sometimes spring in fallow lands;
Weed breeds in gardens; roses grow on thorns.
So, whatsoe'er my Mosby's father was,
Himself is valued gentle by his worth.

MOSBY Ah, how you women can insinuate
And clear a trespass with your sweet-set tongue!
I will forget this quarrel, gentle Alice,
Provided I'll be tempted so no more.

Here enters Bradshaw

ALICE Then with thy lips seal up this new-made match.

MOSBY Soft, Alice, for here comes somebody.

ALICE How now, Bradshaw, what's the news with you?

BRADSHAW I have little news, but here's a letter
That Master Greene impòrtuned me to give you.

ALICE Go in, Bradshaw, call for a cup of beer.
'Tis almost supper time; thou shalt stay with us.

Exit [*Bradshaw*]

Then she reads the letter

'We have missed of our purpose at London, but shall perform it by the way. We thank our neighbour Bradshaw.
Yours,
Richard Greene.'
How likes my love the tenor of this letter?

MOSBY Well, were his date expired and complete!

ALICE Ah, would it were! Then comes my happy hour.
Till then my bliss is mixed with bitter gall.

8.138 **gentles** gentlemen and gentlewomen
8.139 **gentle** honourable (but also kind)
8.141 **fallow** uncultivated
8.142 **Weed** weeds (collective noun)
8.144 **gentle** a gentleman
8.146 **clear a trespass** exonerate
8.150 **Soft** wait
8.153 **impòrtuned** requested
8.160 **tenor** sense
8.161 **his...expired** i.e. if only the letter announced that Arden was dead. Mosby uses the language of finance to link Arden's death to defaulting on a loan.
8.163 **bitter gall** bile, rancour

Come, let us in to shun suspicïon.
MOSBY Ay, to the gates of death to follow thee. *Exeunt*

Sc. 9

Here enter Greene, Will, and Shakebag

SHAKEBAG Come, Will, see thy tools be in a readiness!
Is not thy powder dank, or will thy flint strike fire?
WILL Then ask me if my nose be on my face,
Or whether my tongue be frozen in my mouth.
'Swounds, here's a coil!
You were best swear me on the inter'gatories
How many pistols I have took in hand,
Or whether I love the smell of gunpowder,
Or dare abide the noise the dag will make,
Or will not wink at flashing of the fire.
I pray thee, Shakebag, let this answer thee:
That I have took more purses in this down
Than e'er thou handledst pistols in thy life.
SHAKEBAG Ay, haply thou hast picked more in a throng;
But, should I brag what booties I have took,
I think the overplus that's more than thine
Would mount to a greater sum of money
Than either thou or all thy kin are worth.
'Swounds, I hate them as I hate a toad
That carry a *moschetto* in their tongue

Sc. 9 9.1 **tools** weapons
9.2 **powder** gunpowder
9.2 **dank** wet
9.2 **flint** Flint was used to ignite the gunpowder in a flintlock pistol.
9.5 **coil** fuss
9.6–13 **You...life** Black Will's pronominal movement from the respectful *you* to the disdainful *thou* alerts the audience to the change of relationship between the characters.
9.6 **inter'gatories** interrogatories, legal questions
9.9 **dag** pistol
9.10 **wink** shut my eyes
9.10 **flashing...fire** firing of the gun
9.12 **down** countryside
9.14 **picked** pick-pocketed
9.15 **booties** plunders, spoils
9.16 **overplus** additional
9.19 **toad** loathsome person; servile individual; courtier
9.20 **moschetto** Italian for 'musket'

And scarce a hurting weapon in their hand.
WILL O Greene, intolerable!
It is not for mine honour to bear this.
Why, Shakebag, I did serve the King at Boulogne,
And thou canst brag of nothing that thou hast done.
SHAKEBAG Why, so can Jack of Faversham,
That swoonèd for a fillip on the nose,
When he that gave it him hallowed in his ear,
And he supposed a cannon-bullet hit him.

Then they fight

GREENE I pray you, sirs, list to Aesop's talk:
Whilst two stout dogs were striving for a bone,
There comes a cur and stole it from them both;
So, while you stand striving on these terms of manhood,
Arden escapes us and deceives us all.
SHAKEBAG Why, he begun.
WILL And thou shalt find I'll end.
I do but slip it until better time.
But, if I do forget—

Then he kneels down and holds up his hands to heaven

GREENE Well, take your fittest standings, and once more
Lime your twigs to catch this weary bird.
I'll leave you, and at your dag's discharge
Make towards, like the longing water-dog
That coucheth till the fowling-piece be off,
Then seizeth on the prey with eager mood.

9.26 **Jack of Faversham** *Jack* is an all-purpose name for commoners. Shakebag could mean the common people of Faversham, or more specifically Jack Fitten (2.68).

9.27 **swoonèd for** fainted at

9.27 **fillip** a sharp blow

9.28 **hallowed** hollered, yelled

9.30 **Aesop's talk** Aesop lived in sixth-century BC Greece and supposedly authored over 600 fables.

9.31–2 **Whilst... them both** The story in Aesop's *Fables* involves a lion, a bear, and a fox. As the moral was transmitted in medieval writings, it eventually became a tale of three dogs.

9.31 **stout** brave

9.36 **slip** delay

9.38 **standings** standing-places from which to shoot

9.39 **Lime your twigs** i.e. ready your trap. *Lime* or bird-lime was a viscous resin spread on branches to catch small birds.

9.41 **water-dog** hunting dog trained to retrieve waterfowl

9.42 **coucheth** lies down, remains still

9.42 **fowling-piece** light gun for shooting wild fowl

Ah, might I see him stretching forth his limbs
As I have seen them beat their wings ere now.

SHAKEBAG Why, that thou shalt see if he come this way.

GREENE Yes, that he doth, Shakebag, I warrant thee.
But brawl not when I am gone, in any case.
But, sirs, be sure to speed him when he comes;
And in that hope I'll leave you for an hour. *Exit Greene*

[*Then Will and Shakebag conceal themselves*]

Here enter Arden, Franklin, and Michael

MICHAEL 'Twere best that I went back to Rochester.
The horse halts downright; it were not good
He travelled in such pain to Faversham.
Removing of a shoe may haply help it.

ARDEN Well, get you back to Rochester; but, sirrah, see
Ye overtake us ere we come to Rainham Down,
For it will be very late ere we get home.

MICHAEL [*aside*] Ay, God he knows, and so doth Will and Shakebag,
That thou shalt never go further than that down;
And therefore have I pricked the horse on purpose,
Because I would not view the massacre. *Exit Michael*

ARDEN Come, Master Franklin, onwards with your tale.

FRANKLIN I assure you, sir, you task me much.
A heavy blood is gathered at my heart,
And on the sudden is my wind so short
As hindereth the passage of my speech.
So fierce a qualm yet ne'er assailèd me.

ARDEN Come, Master Franklin, let us go on softly.

9.45 **them** i.e. waterfowl
9.45 **beat their wings** newly killed but are still beating their wings
9.48 **in any case** whatever you do
9.49 **speed** i.e. kill
9.52 **halts downright** limps badly
9.53 **travelled** (punning on the sense 'travailed', laboured)
9.54 **shoe** horseshoe
9.56 **overtake** catch up with
9.58 **God he knows** (proverbial: 'God he knows, not I' (Dent, G189.1))
9.60 **pricked** stabbed
9.62 **Master...tale** A glance at Chaucer's *Canterbury Tales*, whose pilgrims travelled on the same road. The Host says to the Franklin 'Telle on thy tale withouten wordes mo' ('Squire's Tale', 702).
9.64 **heavy blood** harsh feeling or disposition
9.65 **wind** breath
9.67 **qualm** spasm of sickness, pang of misgiving

The annoyance of the dust or else some meat
You ate at dinner cannot brook you.
I have been often so and soon amended.

FRANKLIN Do you remember where my tale did leave?

ARDEN Ay, where the gentleman did check his wife.

FRANKLIN She being reprehended for the fact,
Witness produced that took her with the deed,
Her glove brought in which there she left behind,
And many other assurèd arguments,
Her husband asked her whether it were not so.

ARDEN Her answer then? I wonder how she looked,
Having forsworn it with such vehement oaths,
And at the instant so approved upon her.

FRANKLIN First did she cast her eyes down to the earth,
Watching the drops that fell amain from thence;
Then softly draws she forth her handkerchief,
And modestly she wipes her tear-stained face;
Then 'hemmed' she out (to clear her voice, should seem),
And with a majesty addressed herself
To encounter all their accusatïons.
Pardon me, Master Arden, I can no more;
This fighting at my heart makes short my wind.

ARDEN Come, we are almost now at Rainham Down.
Your pretty tale beguiles the weary way;
I would you were in state to tell it out.

SHAKEBAG [*aside to Will*] Stand close, Will: I hear them coming.

Here enters Lord Cheyne with his men

WILL [*aside to Shakebag*] Stand to it, Shakebag, and be resolute.

LORD CHEYNE Is it so near night as it seems,
Or will this black-faced evening have a shower?—
What, Master Arden? You are well met.

9.70 **brook** tolerate, does not agree with
9.73 **check** reprimand
9.74 **fact** wrongdoing
9.75 **took...deed** i.e. caught her in the act
9.81 **approved upon** demonstrated against
9.83 **amain** with vigour
9.86 **hemmed** gave a short, sharp cough
9.92 **beguiles** diverts attention from
9.93 **would** i.e. wish

I have longed this fortnight's day to speak with you.
You are a stranger, man, in the Isle of Sheppey.

ARDEN Your honour's always, bound to do you service.

LORD CHEYNE Come you from London? and ne'er a man with you?

ARDEN My man's coming after,
But here's my honest friend that came along with me.

LORD CHEYNE [*to Franklin*] My Lord Protector's man, I take you to be.

FRANKLIN Ay, my good lord, and highly bound to you.

LORD CHEYNE You and your friend come home and sup with me.

ARDEN I beseech your honour pardon me;
I have made a promise to a gentleman,
My honest friend, to meet him at my house.
The occasion is great, or else would I wait on you.

LORD CHEYNE Will you come tomorrow and dine with me,
And bring your honest friend along with you?
I have divers matters to talk with you about.

ARDEN Tomorrow we'll wait upon your honour.

LORD CHEYNE [*to his men*] One of you stay my horse at the top of the hill. [*Exit a man*]
What, Black Will, for whose purse wait you?
Thou wilt be hanged in Kent when all is done.

WILL Not hanged, God save your honour.
I am your beadsman, bound to pray for you.

LORD CHEYNE I think thou ne'er said'st prayer in all thy life.
[*To his men*] One of you give him a crown.
[*To Will*] And, sirrah, leave this kind of life.
If thou be'st 'tainted for a penny matter
And come in question, surely thou wilt truss.—
Come, Master Arden, let us be going;
Your way and mine lies four mile together.

Exeunt. Manent Black Will and Shakebag

WILL The devil break all your necks at four miles' end!

9.104 **honest friend** i.e. Franklin
9.120 **beadsman** one that prays for others; servant
9.124 **'tainted** accused
9.124 **penny** i.e. trivial
9.125 **truss** be trussed up and hanged

'Swounds, I could kill myself for very anger!
His lordship chops me in
Even when my dag was levelled at his heart.
I would his crown were molten down his throat!

SHAKEBAG Arden, thou hast wondrous holy luck.
Did ever man escape as thou hast done?
Well, I'll discharge my pistol at the sky,
For by this bullet Arden might not die.

[Then Shakebag fires his pistol]

Here enters Greene

GREENE What, is he down? Is he dispatched?!

SHAKEBAG Ay, in health towards Faversham, to shame us all.

GREENE The devil he is! Why, sirs, how escaped he?

SHAKEBAG When we were ready to shoot,
Comes my Lord Cheyne to prevent his death.

GREENE The Lord of Heaven hath preservèd him.

WILL The Lord of Heaven?—a fig! The Lord Cheyne hath preserved him, and bids him to a feast to his house at Shurland.
But by the way once more I'll meet with him,
And if all the Cheynes in the world say no,
I'll have a bullet in his breast tomorrow.
Therefore come, Greene, and let us to Faversham.

GREENE Ay, and excuse ourselves to Mistress Arden.
O, how she'll chafe when she hears of this!

SHAKEBAG Why I'll warrant you she'll think we dare not do it.

WILL Why, then let us go, and tell her all the matter,
And plot the news to cut him off tomorrow. *Exeunt.*

9.130 **chops me in** intervenes
9.136 **For** Because
9.136 **might** could
9.138 **Faversham** The line puns on the sixteenth-century pronunciation, 'Fevershame'.
9.143 **a fig!** (an exclamation signifying disdain)
9.144 **Shurland** (the residence of Lord Cheyne, on the island of Sheppey, not far from Faversham)
9.150 **chafe** be angry
9.153 **plot the news** create a new plan

Sc. 10

Here enter Arden and his wife [Alice,] Franklin, and Michael

ARDEN See how the Hours, the guardïans of heaven's gate,
Have by their toil removed the darksome clouds,
That Sol may well discern the trampled pace
Wherein he wont to guide his golden car.
The season fits. Come, Franklin, let's away.

ALICE I thought you did pretend some special hunt
That made you thus cut short the time of rest.

ARDEN It was no chase that made me rise so early
But, as I told thee yesternight, to go
To the Isle of Sheppey, there to dine with my Lord Cheyne;
For so his honour late commanded me.

ALICE Ay, such kind husbands seldom want excuses;
Home is a wild cat to a wand'ring wit.
The time hath been—would God it were not past!—
That honour's title nor a lord's command
Could once have drawn you from these arms of mine.
But my deserts or your desires decay,
Or both; yet if true love may seem desert,
I merit still to have thy company.

FRANKLIN Why, I pray you, sir, let her go along with us.
I am sure his honour will welcome her,
And us the more for bringing her along.

ARDEN Content. [*To Michael*] Sirrah, saddle your mistress' nag.

ALICE No, beggèd favour merits little thanks.
If I should go, our house would run away
Or else be stol'n; therefore I'll stay behind.

ARDEN Nay, see how mistaking you are! I pray thee, go.

Sc. 10 10.1 **Hours...gate** In classical mythology, the Hours were daughters of Jupiter and Themis. They were thought to guard the gate of Olympus and supervise the change of seasons.
10.3 **Sol** (personification of the sun)
10.3 **discern** (the sun is rising)
10.3 **pace** path
10.4 **wont** is accustomed to
10.4 **car** chariot
10.6 **pretend** intend
10.11 **late** lately
10.12 **want** lack
10.13 **Home...wit** home is unpleasant to those with a fickle or capricious nature
10.17 **deserts** qualities
10.18 **desert** deserving

ALICE No, no, not now.

ARDEN Then let me leave thee satisfied in this,
That time, nor place, nor persons alter me,
But that I hold thee dearer than my life.

ALICE That will be seen by your quick return.

ARDEN And that shall be ere night an if I live.
Farewell, sweet Alice. We mind to sup with thee. *Exit Alice*

FRANKLIN Come, Michael, are our horses ready?

MICHAEL Ay, your horse are ready, but I am not ready, for I have lost my purse with six-and-thirty shillings in it, with taking up of my master's nag.

FRANKLIN [*to Arden*] Why, I pray you, let us go before,
Whilst he stays behind to seek his purse.

ARDEN [*to Michael*] Go to, sirrah!
See you follow us to the Isle of Sheppey,
To my Lord Cheyne's, where we mean to dine.

Exeunt Arden and Franklin. Manet Michael

MICHAEL So, fair weather after you!—for before you lies Black Will and Shakebag in the broom close, too close for you. They'll be your ferrymen to your long home.

Here enters [*Clarke*] *the painter*

But who is this? The painter, my corrival, that would needs win Mistress Susan.

CLARKE How now, Michael? How doth my mistress and all at home?

MICHAEL Who? Susan Mosby? She's your mistress, too?

CLARKE Ay, how doth she and all the rest?

MICHAEL All's well but Susan; she is sick.

CLARKE Sick? Of what disease?

MICHAEL Of a great fere.

CLARKE A fear of what?

10.33 **an if** if
10.37 **taking up** lodging in stalls
10.45 **broom close** boundary hedge of broom
10.46 **ferrymen** (comparing them to Charon, the ferryman who transported souls across the river Styx)
10.46 **your long home** the place where you will reside the longest: death, the afterlife
10.47 **corrival** co-rival
10.54 **fere** spouse (but misinterpreted by Clarke as 'fear')

MICHAEL A great fever.

CLARKE A fever? God forbid!

MICHAEL Yes, faith, and of a lurdan, too, as big as yourself.

CLARKE O Michael, the spleen prickles you. Go to; you carry an eye over Mistress Susan.

MICHAEL Ay, faith, to keep her from the painter.

CLARKE Why more from a painter than from a serving-creature like yourself?

MICHAEL Because you painters make but a painting-table of a pretty wench, and spoil her beauty with blotting.

CLARKE What mean you by that?

MICHAEL Why, that you painters paint lambs in the lining of wenches' petticoats, and we servingmen put horns to them to make them become sheep.

CLARKE Such another word will cost you a cuff or a knock.

MICHAEL What, with a dagger made of a pencil? Faith, 'tis too weak, and therefore thou too weak to win Susan.

CLARKE Would Susan's love lay upon this stroke!

Then he breaks Michael's head

Here enter Mosby, Greene, and Alice

ALICE I'll lay my life, this is for Susan's love.
[*To Michael*] Stayed you behind your master to this end?
Have you no other time to brabble in
But now when serious matters are in hand?—
Say, Clarke, hast thou done the thing thou promised?

CLARKE Ay, here it is: the very touch is death.

10.58 **lurdan** vagabond (but playing on *fever-lurdan* , the disease of being lazy)
10.59 **spleen** In early modern humoral theory, the spleen was the seat of melancholy (and also laughter). Here, *spleen* means a sudden outburst of emotion.
10.59 **prickles** stings, irritates
10.59–60 **carry an eye over** watch closely
10.64 **painting-table** i.e. a painting
10.65 **blotting** poor technique; effacement
10.68 **horns** penises; the horns of the cuckold
10.69 **make them become sheep** lead them astray; make them obedient (to their desires)
10.70 **cuff** blow
10.71 **dagger...pencil** small penis; a paintbrush as a dagger, with additional connotations of diminished or slackened male genitalia
10.76 **brabble** brawl
10.78 **the thing** i.e. the poisoned crucifix

[*Then Clarke shows the poisoned crucifix*]

ALICE Then this, I hope, if all the rest do fail,
Will catch Master Arden
And make him wise in death that lived a fool.
[*To Mosby*] Why should he thrust his sickle in our corn,
Or what hath he to do with thee, my love,
Or govern me that am to rule myself?
Forsooth, for credit sake, I must leave thee.
Nay, he must leave to live, that we may love—
May live, my love: for what is life but love?
And love shall last as long as life remains,
And life shall end before my love depart.

MOSBY Why, what's love, without true constancy?
Like to a pillar built of many stones,
Yet neither with good mortar well compact,
Nor cèment to fasten it in the joints,
But that it shakes with every blast of wind
And, being touched, straight falls unto the earth
And buries all his haughty pride in dust.
No, let our love be rocks of adamant,
Which time nor place nor tempest can asunder.

GREENE Mosby, leave protestations now,
And let us bethink us what we have to do.
Black Will and Shakebag I have placed
In the broom close, watching Arden's coming.
Let's to them and see what they have done. *Exeunt*

Sc. 11

Here enter Arden and Franklin

ARDEN O ferryman, where art thou?

Here enters the Ferryman

FERRYMAN Here, here! Go before to the boat, and I will follow you.

10.83 **thrust...corn** impede, interfere. The phrase is proverbial: 'Put not thy sickle in another man's corn' (Dent, S420).

10.86 **Forsooth** certainly

10.93 **compact** composed

10.98 **rocks of adamant** i.e. exceptionally strong

10.99 **asunder** separate

ARDEN We have great haste; I pray thee come away.

FERRYMAN Fie, what a mist is here!

ARDEN This mist, my friend, is mystical,
Like to a good companion's smoky brain,
That was half-drowned with new ale overnight.

FERRYMAN 'Twere pity but his skull were opened to make more chimney room.

FRANKLIN Friend, what's thy opinion of this mist?

FERRYMAN I think 'tis like to a curst wife in a little house, that never leaves her husband till she have driven him out at doors with a wet pair of eyes. Then looks he as if his house were afire, or some of his friends dead.

ARDEN Speaks thou this of thine own experience?

FERRYMAN Perhaps ay, perhaps no; for my wife is as other women are, that is to say, governed by the moon.

FRANKLIN By the moon? How, I pray thee?

FERRYMAN Nay, thereby lies a bargain, and you shall not have it fresh and fasting.

ARDEN Yes, I pray thee, good ferryman.

FERRYMAN Then for this once: let it be midsummer moon, but yet my wife has another moon.

FRANKLIN Another moon?

FERRYMAN Ay, and it hath influences and eclipses.

ARDEN Why, then, by this reckoning you sometimes play the man in the moon.

FERRYMAN Ay, but you had not best to meddle with that moon, lest I scratch you by the face with my bramble-bush.

ARDEN I am almost stifled with this fog. Come, let's away.

Sc. 11 11.5 **mystical** opaque, thick (with a pun on *mist*)

11.6 **smoky** foggy; disagreeable

11.7 **new ale** New (or freshly brewed) ale was stronger than ordinary ale.

11.11 **curst** irritable

11.17 **governed by the moon** inconstant. Alludes to the proverb: 'As changeful as the moon' (Dent, M1111); here referring to the menstrual cycle.

11.20 **fresh and fasting** so easily; for nothing

11.22 **midsummer moon** i.e. a time of lunacy

11.23 **another moon** i.e. her genitals

11.25 **it... eclipses** i.e. her genitals are affected by the intervention of other bodies

11.26–7 **the man in the moon** i.e. have sex with her

FRANKLIN And, sirrah, as we go, let us have some more of your bold yeomanry.

FERRYMAN Nay, by my troth, sir, but flat knavery. *Exeunt*

Sc. 12

Here enter Will at one door and Shakebag at another

SHAKEBAG O Will, where art thou?

WILL Here, Shakebag, almost in hell's mouth, where I cannot see my way for smoke.

SHAKEBAG I pray thee, speak still that we may meet by the sound, for I shall fall into some ditch or other unless my feet see better than my eyes.

WILL Didst thou ever see better weather to run away with another man's wife or play with a wench at pot-finger?

SHAKEBAG No; this were a fine world for chandlers, if this weather would last, for then a man should never dine nor sup without candle-light. But sirrah Will, what horses are those that passed?

WILL Why, didst thou hear any?

SHAKEBAG Ay, that I did.

WILL My life for thine, 'twas Arden and his companion, and then all our labour's lost.

SHAKEBAG Nay, say not so, for, if it be they, they may haply lose their way as we have done, and then we may chance meet with them.

WILL Come, let us go on like a couple of blind pilgrims.

Then Shakebag falls into a ditch

SHAKEBAG Help, Will, help! I am almost drowned.

Here enters the Ferryman

FERRYMAN Who's that that calls for help?

WILL 'Twas none here; 'twas thou thyself.

11.32 **yeomanry** simple, homely speech

Sc. 12 12.2 **hell's mouth** (the entrance to hell, but also a theatrical set; here probably also alluding to the open trapdoor)

12.3 **smoke** i.e. mist

12.8 **pot-finger** a game involving making popping sounds by rapidly removing a finger from the corner of the mouth. Black Will suggests something bawdier here.

12.9 **chandlers** candle makers

FERRYMAN I came to help him that called for help. Why, how now? Who is this that's in the ditch? [*To Shakebag*] You are well enough served to go without a guide such weather as this!

WILL Sirrah, what companies hath passed your ferry this morning?

FERRYMAN None but a couple of gentlemen that went to dine at my Lord Cheyne's.

WILL Shakebag, did not I tell thee as much?

FERRYMAN Why, sir, will you have any letters carried to them?

WILL No, sir; get you gone.

FERRYMAN Did you ever see such a mist as this?

WILL No, nor such a fool as will rather be hocked than get his way.

FERRYMAN Why, sir, this is no Hock Monday; you are deceived.

[*Then he helps Shakebag out of the ditch*]

What's his name, I pray you, sir?

SHAKEBAG His name is Black Will.

FERRYMAN I hope to see him one day hanged upon a hill.

Exit Ferryman

SHAKEBAG See how the sun hath cleared the foggy mist.
Now we have missed the mark of our intent.

Here enter Greene, Mosby, and Alice

MOSBY Black Will and Shakebag, what make you here?
What, is the deed done? Is Arden dead?

WILL What could a blinded man perform in arms?
Saw you not how till now the sky was dark,
That neither horse nor man could be discerned?
Yet did we hear their horses as they passed.

GREENE Have they escaped you then and passed the ferry?

SHAKEBAG Ay, for a while; but here we two will stay
And at their coming back meet with them once more.
'Swounds, I was ne'er so toiled in all my life
In following so slight a task as this.

12.25 **companies** groups of people
12.32 **hocked** houghed, hamstrung
12.33 **Hock Monday** (or Hocktide, a festival observed on the second Monday after Easter where women customarily coerced men into paying a ransom by restraining them)
12.48 **toiled** drained, worn out

MOSBY [*to Shakebag*] How cam'st thou so bewrayed?

WILL With making false footing in the dark.
He needs would follow them without a guide.

[*Then Alice gives money to Will and Shakebag*]

ALICE Here's to pay for a fire and good cheer.
Get you to Faversham to the Flower-de-Luce
And rest yourselves until some other time.

GREENE Let me along; it most concerns my state.

WILL Ay, Mistress Arden, this will serve the turn
In case we fall into a second fog.

Exeunt Greene, Will, and Shakebag

MOSBY These knaves will never do it; let us give it over.

ALICE First tell me how you like my new device:
Soon, when my husband is returning back,
You and I, both marching arm in arm
Like loving friends, we'll meet him on the way
And boldly beard and brave him to his teeth.
When words grow hot and blows begin to rise,
I'll call those cutters forth your tenement,
Who, in a manner to take up the fray,
Shall wound my husband Hornsby to the death.

MOSBY Ah, fine device! Why, this deserves a kiss.

[*Then he kisses her.*] *Exeunt*

Sc. 13

Here enter Dick Reede and a Sailor

SAILOR Faith, Dick Reede, it is to little end.
His conscience is too liberal and he too niggardly
To part from anything may do thee good.

REEDE He is coming from Shorlan as I understand.
Here I'll intercept him, for at his house
He never will vouchsafe to speak with me.

12.50 **bewrayed** dirtied
12.56 **Let me along** let me go along (with them), let me join in
12.64 **beard and brave** insult, provoke
12.66 **forth** out
12.66 **tenement** dwelling
12.68 **Hornsby** i.e. the cuckold

Sc. 13 13.1 **end** purpose
13.6 **vouchsafe** agree

If prayers and fair entreaties will not serve
Or make no batt'ry in his flinty breast,

Here enter Franklin, Arden, and Michael

I'll curse the carl and see what that will do.
See where he comes to further my intent.—
Master Arden, I am now bound to the sea.
My coming to you was about the plot of ground
Which wrongfully you detain from me.
Although the rent of it be very small,
Yet will it help my wife and childëren,
Which here I leave in Faversham, God knows,
Needy and bare. For Christ's sake, let them have it.

ARDEN Franklin, hearest thou this fellow speak?
That which he craves I dearly bought of him,
Although the rent of it was ever mine.
[*To Reede*] Sirrah, you that ask these questïons,
If with thy clamorous impeaching tongue
Thou rail on me, as I have heard thou dost,
I'll lay thee up so close a twelvemonth's day
As thou shalt neither see the sun nor moon.
Look to it, for, as surely as I live,
I'll banish pity if thou use me thus.

REEDE What, wilt thou do me wrong and threat me too?
Nay, then, I'll tempt thee, Arden: do thy worst.
God, I beseech thee, show some miracle
On thee or thine in plaguing thee for this.
That plot of ground which thou detains from me—
I speak it in an agony of spirit—
Be ruinous and fatal unto thee!
Either there be butchered by thy dearest friends,
Or else be brought for men to wonder at,
Or thou or thine miscarry in that place,
Or there run mad and end thy cursèd days.

13.8 **batt'ry** attack, assailment
13.9 **carl** miser
13.22 **clamorous impeaching tongue** vociferous and accusatory speech
13.24 **lay thee up** imprison you
13.27 **use** treat
13.29 **tempt** provoke
13.37 **miscarry** disaster

FRANKLIN Fie, bitter knave, bridle thine envious tongue;
For curses are like arrows shot upright,
Which, falling down, light on the shooter's head.

REEDE Light where they will! Were I upon the sea,
As oft I have in many a bitter storm,
And saw a dreadful southern flaw at hand,
The pilot quaking at the doubtful storm,
And all the sailors praying on their knees,
Even in that fearful time would I fall down
And ask of God: 'whate'er betide of me,
Vengeance on Arden, or some misevent
To show the world what wrong the carl hath done.'
This charge I'll leave with my distressful wife;
My children shall be taught such prayers as these.
And thus I go, but leave my curse with thee.

Exeunt Reede and Sailor

ARDEN It is the railingest knave in Christendom,
And oftentimes the villain will be mad.
It greatly matters not what he says,
But I assure you I ne'er did him wrong.

FRANKLIN I think so, Master Arden.

ARDEN Now that our horses are gone home before,
My wife may haply meet me on the way;
For God knows she is grown passing kind of late
And greatly changèd from the old humour
Of her wonted frowardness,
And seeks by fair means to redeem old faults.

FRANKLIN Happy the change that alters for the best!
But see in any case you make no speech
Of the cheer we had at my Lord Cheyne's
Although most bounteous and liberal,
For that will make her think herself more wronged

13.39 **bridle** restrain
13.39 **envious** vicious, resentful
13.40–1 **curses...head** (proverbial: 'Curses return upon the heads of those that curse' (Dent, C924))
13.44 **flaw** squall
13.45 **doubtful** ominous, feared
13.49 **misevent** misfortune
13.54 **railingest** most abusive, obnoxious
13.61 **passing** very
13.62 **old humour** previous disposition
13.63 **wonted frowardness** habitual difficulty
13.67 **cheer** hospitality

In that we did not carry her along;
For sure she grieved that she was left behind.

ARDEN Come, Franklin, let us strain to mend our pace
And take her unawares playing the cook;

Here enter Alice and Mosby [*arm in arm*]

For I believe she'll strive to mend our cheer.

FRANKLIN Why, there's no better creatures in the world
Than women are—when they are in good humours.

ARDEN Who is that? Mosby? What, so familiar?
Injurious strumpet and thou ribald knave,
Untwine those arms.

ALICE Ay, with a sugared kiss let them untwine.

[*Then she kisses Mosby*]

ARDEN Ah, Mosby! Perjured beast! Bear this and all!

MOSBY And yet no hornèd beast: the horns are thine.

FRANKLIN O monstrous! Nay, then, 'tis time to draw.

[*Then Arden and Franklin draw their swords*]

ALICE Help! Help! They murder my husband.

Here enter Will and Shakebag

SHAKEBAG 'Swounds, who injures Master Mosby?
[*Then they fight, and Shakebag and Mosby are hurt*]
Help, Will! I am hurt.

MOSBY I may thank you, Mistress Arden, for this wound.
Exeunt Mosby, Will, and Shakebag

ALICE Ah, Arden, what folly blinded thee?
Ah, jealous harebrain man, what hast thou done?
When we, to welcome thee, intended sport,
Came lovingly to meet thee on thy way,
Thou drew'st thy sword, enraged with jealousy,
And hurt thy friend whose thoughts were free from harm,
All for a worthless kiss and joining arms,

13.72 **mend** increase
13.78 **strumpet** whore
13.78 **ribald** low-born; unpleasant
13.81 **Bear...all** Anyone who tolerates this will tolerate anything! The expression is proverbial (Dent, A172).
13.82 **hornèd beast** i.e. cuckold
13.89 **harebrain** reckless

Both done but merrily to try thy patience—
And me unhappy that devised the jest,
Which, though begun in sport, yet ends in blood.

FRANKLIN Marry, God defend me from such a jest!

ALICE Couldst thou not see us friendly smile on thee
When we joined arms and when I kissed his cheek?
Hast thou not lately found me overkind?
Didst thou not hear me cry they murder thee?
Called I not help to set my husband free?
No, ears and all were witched. Ah me accursed,
To link in liking with a frantic man!
Henceforth I'll be thy slave, no more thy wife;
For with that name I never shall content thee.
If I be merry, thou straightways thinks me light;
If sad, thou say'st the sullens trouble me;
If well attired, thou thinks I will be gadding;
If homely, I seem sluttish in thine eye.
Thus am I still, and shall be while I die,
Poor wench abused by thy misgovernment.

ARDEN But is it for truth that neither thou nor he
Intendedst malice in your misdemeanour?

ALICE The heavens can witness of our harmless thoughts.

ARDEN Then pardon me, sweet Alice, and forgive this fault.
Forget but this and never see the like.
Impose me penance, and I will perform it;
For in thy discontent I find a death,
A death tormenting more than death itself.

ALICE Nay, hadst thou loved me as thou dost pretend,
Thou wouldst have marked the speeches of thy friend,
Who going wounded from the place, he said
His skin was pierced only through my device.

13.104 **witched** bewitched (influenced by jealousy)
13.105 **link in liking** be companioned
13.109 **sullens** sombre moods, sulking
13.110 **gadding** wandering
13.111 **homely** plainly or unpretentiously dressed
13.111 **sluttish** repulsive
13.112 **still** always
13.113 **misgovernment** negligence

And if sad sorrow taint thee for this fault,
Thou wouldst have followed him, and seen him dressed,
And cried him mercy whom thou hast misdone;
Ne'er shall my heart be eased till this be done.

ARDEN Content thee, sweet Alice, thou shalt have thy will,
Whate'er it be. For that I injured thee
And wronged my friend, shame scourgeth my offence.
Come thou thyself, and go along with me,
And be a mediator 'twixt us two.

FRANKLIN Why, Master Arden, know you what you do?
Will you follow him that hath dishonoured you?

ALICE Why, canst thou prove I have been disloyal?

FRANKLIN Why, Mosby taunts your husband with the horn.

ALICE Ay, after he had rèviled him
By the injurious name of 'perjured beast'.
He knew no wrong could spite a jealous man
More than the hateful naming of the horn.

FRANKLIN Suppose 'tis true, yet is it dangerous
To follow him whom he hath lately hurt.

ALICE A fault confessed is more than half amends,
But men of such ill spirit as yourself
Work crosses and debates 'twixt man and wife.

ARDEN I pray thee, gentle Franklin, hold thy peace;
I know my wife counsels me for the best.
I'll seek out Mosby where his wound is dressed,
And salve his hapless quarrel if I may. *Exeunt Arden and Alice*

FRANKLIN He whom the devil drives must go perforce.
Poor gentleman, how soon he is bewitched!
And yet, because his wife is the instrument,
His friends must not be lavish in their speech. *Exit Franklin*

13.127 **dressed** treated, bandaged
13.128 **misdone** injured
13.132 **scourgeth** punishes
13.145 **A...amends** (proverbial: 'Confession of a fault is half amends' (Dent, C589))
13.147 **crosses** conflicts
13.151 **salve** soothe
13.151 **hapless** unlucky
13.152 **perforce** by necessity
13.155 **lavish** excessive, unrestrained

Sc. 14

Here enter Will, Shakebag [wounded], and Greene

WILL Sirrah Greene, when was I so long in killing a man?

GREENE I think we shall never do it. Let us give it over.

SHAKEBAG Nay. 'Swounds, we'll kill him though we be hanged at his door for our labour.

WILL Thou knowest, Greene, that I have lived in London this twelve years, where I have made some go upon wooden legs for taking the wall on me, divers with silver noses for saying, 'There goes Black Will.' I have cracked as many blades as thou hast done nuts.

GREENE O monstrous lie!

WILL Faith, in a manner I have. The bawdy-houses have paid me tribute: there durst not a whore set up unless she have agreed with me first for opening her shop windows. For a cross word of a tapster I have pierced one barrel after another with my dagger and held him by the ears till all his beer hath run out. In Thames Street a brewer's cart was like to have run over me; I made no more ado but went to the clerk and cut all the notches off his tallies and beat them about his head. I and my company have taken the constable from his watch and carried him about the fields on a cowl-staff. I have broken a sergeant's head with his own mace, and bailed whom I list with my sword and buckler. All the tenpenny alehouse-keepers would stand every morning with a quart pot in his hand, saying, 'Will it please your worship drink?' He that had not done so had been sure to have had his

Sc. 14 14.3–4 **hanged at his door** i.e. captured, executed

14.6 **wooden legs** i.e. crutches

14.6–7 **taking the wall** walking close to the wall (where it is clean) and forcing me to walk in the gutter (the dirtiest part of the street)

14.7 **silver noses** i.e. prosthetic noses

14.10 **bawdy-houses** i.e. whore houses

14.11 **set up** marketing her services

14.12 **for...shop windows** before taking customers; before opening her legs, where *shop windows* is a metaphor for the labia

14.12 **cross** oppositional, unfavourable

14.16 **tallies** a tally was a wooden stick on which *notches* were made to record debts and payments.

14.19 **cowl-staff** a heavy stick used to carry loads

14.19 **sergeant's** The sergeant was responsible for arresting criminals and bringing them to trial.

14.20 **mace** staff of office

14.20 **list** wanted

14.20 **buckler** small shield

14.21 **tenpenny alehouse-keepers** owners of taverns where a quart of beer was sold for tenpence

sign pulled down and his lattice borne away the next night. To conclude, what have I not done? Yet cannot do this! Doubtless he is preserved by miracle.

Here enter Alice and Michael

GREENE Hence, Will! Here comes Mistress Arden.

ALICE Ah, gentle Michael, art thou sure they're friends?

MICHAEL Why, I saw them when they both shook hands.
When Mosby bled, he even wept for sorrow,
And railed on Franklin that was cause of all.
No sooner came the surgeon in at doors
But my master took to his purse, and gave him money—
And, to conclude, sent me to bring you word
That Mosby, Franklin, Bradshaw, Adam Fowle,
With divers of his neighbours and his friends,
Will come and sup with you at our house this night.

ALICE Ah, gentle Michael! Run thou back again,
And when my husband walks into the fair,
Bid Mosby steal from him and come to me.
And this night shall thou and Susan be made sure.

MICHAEL I'll go tell him.

ALICE And, as thou goest, tell John cook of our guests,
And bid him lay it on; spare for no cost. *Exit Michael*

WILL Nay, an there be such cheer, we will bid ourselves.

[*Then they approach her*]

Mistress Arden, Dick Greene and I do mean to sup with you.

ALICE And welcome shall you be. Ah gentlemen,
How missed you of your purpose yesternight?

GREENE 'Twas long of Shakebag, that unlucky villain.

SHAKEBAG Thou dost me wrong. I did as much as any.

WILL Nay, then, Mistress Alice, I'll tell you how it was. When he should have locked with both his hilts, he in a bravery flourished

14.24 **lattice** Alehouses often displayed red or green latticework.
14.26 **he** i.e. Arden
14.39 **fair** (town gathering in celebration of St Valentine's Day)
14.43 **John cook** i.e. John the cook
14.45 **bid** invite
14.49 **long of** on account of
14.52 **locked...hilts** engaged Arden in hand-to-hand combat
14.52 **in a bravery** with bravado
14.52 **flourished** waved (his sword)

over his head. With that comes Franklin at him lustily and hurts the slave. With that he slinks away.
Now his way had been to have come in hand and feet, one and two round at his costard. He like a fool bears his sword point half a yard out of danger. I lie here for my life. If the devil come, and he have no more strength than fence, he shall never beat me from this ward. I'll stand to it, a buckler in a skilful hand, is as good as a castle. Nay, 'tis better than a sconce, for I have tried it.
Mosby, perceiving this, began to faint.
With that comes Arden with his arming-sword
And thrust him through the shoulder in a trice.

ALICE Ay, but I wonder why you both stood still.

WILL Faith, I was so amazed I could not strike.

ALICE Ah, sirs, had he yesternight been slain,
For every drop of his detested blood
I would have crammed in angels in thy fist—
And kissed thee too, and hugged thee in my arms.

WILL Patient yourself, we cannot help it now.
Greene and we two will dog him through the fair,
And stab him in the crowd and steal away,

Here enters Mosby [with his arm and shoulder bandaged]

ALICE It is unpossible. But here comes he
That will, I hope, invent some surer means.
Sweet Mosby, hide thy arm: it kills my heart.

MOSBY Ay, Mistress Arden, this is your favour.

ALICE Ah, say not so, for when I saw thee hurt,
I could have took the weapon thou lett'st fall
And run at Arden—for I have sworn
That these mine eyes (offended with his sight)

14.55 **come in** make a pass or home-thrust, to get within the opponent's guard
14.56 **costard** head
14.57 **I lie here** I depend on this (fencing) position
14.58 **fence** fencing
14.59 **ward** defensive position
14.60 **sconce** small fort
14.61 **faint** cower
14.62 **with...arming-sword** armed with a sword
14.63 **in a trice** in an instant
14.65 **amazed** dumbfounded
14.68 **angels** coins, payment
14.70 **Patient yourself** be patient
14.71 **dog** hunt
14.76 **favour** gift

Shall never close till Arden's be shut up.
This night I rose and walked about the chamber,
And twice or thrice I thought to have murdered him—

MOSBY What, in the night? Then had we been undone.

ALICE Why, how long shall he live?

MOSBY Faith, Alice, no longer than this night.
Black Will and Shakebag, will you two
Perform the complot that I have laid?

WILL Ay, or else think me as a villain.

GREENE And rather than you shall want, I'll help myself.

MOSBY You, Master Greene, shall single Franklin forth
And hold him with a long tale of strange news,
That he may not come home till supper time.
I'll fetch Master Arden home, and we (like friends)
Will play a game or two at tables here.

ALICE But what of all this? How shall he be slain?

MOSBY Why, Black Will and Shakebag, locked within the counting-house,
Shall, at a certain watchword given, rush forth.

WILL What shall the watchword be?

MOSBY 'Now I can take you'—that shall be the word.
But come not forth before in any case.

WILL I warrant you. But who shall lock me in?

ALICE That will I do. Thou'st keep the key thyself.

MOSBY Come, Master Greene, go you along with me.
See all things ready, Alice, against we come.

ALICE Take no care for that. Send you him home;
And if he ere go forth again, blame me.

Exeunt Mosby and Greene

Come, Black Will, that in mine eyes art fair;
Next unto Mosby do I honour thee.

14.90 **want** fail
14.95 **tables** backgammon
14.97 **counting-house** private office
14.98 **watchword** a word or phrase used as a password or signal
14.100 **take you** i.e. win the game (with the implied suggestion of taking Arden's life)
14.105 **against we come** by the time we arrive
14.106 **Take...that** leave that to me

Instead of fair words and large promises,
My hands shall play you golden harmony.
How like you this? Say, will you do it, sirs?

WILL Ay, and that bravely too. Mark my device.
Place Mosby, being a stranger, in a chair,
And let your husband sit upon a stool,
That I may come behind him cunningly
And with a towel pull him to the ground,
Then stab him till his flesh be as a sieve.
That done, bear him behind the Abbey,
That those that find him murdered may suppose
Some slave or other killed him for his gold.

ALICE A fine device! You shall have twenty pound—

[*Then she gives Will and Shakebag twenty pound*]

And when he is dead, you shall have forty more.
And, lest you might be suspected staying here,
Michael shall saddle you two lusty geldings.
Ride whither you will, to Scotland or to Wales.
I'll see you shall not lack where'er you be.

WILL Such words would make one kill a thousand men!
Give me the key. Which is the counting-house?

[*Then Alice gives him the key and points to the counting-house door*]

ALICE Here would I stay and still encourage you,
But that I know how resolute you are.

SHAKEBAG Tush! You are too faint-hearted; we must do it.

ALICE But Mosby will be there, whose very looks
Will add unwonted courage to my thought
And make me the first that shall adventure on him.

WILL Tush, get you gone! 'Tis we must do the deed.

14.111 **hands...golden harmony** provide you with payment

14.113 **bravely** happily

14.114 **chair** Chairs were rare and expensive household items, and they were usually reserved for the principal male of the household.

14.125 **geldings** castrated horses. Castrating a horse makes it more obedient and quiet.

14.127 **lack** i.e. be without what's owed to you

14.135 **adventure on** i.e. overtake, attack

When this door opens next, look for his death.
[*Exeunt Will and Shakebag through the counting-house door*]

ALICE Ah, would he now were here, that it might open!
I shall no more be closed in Arden's arms,
That, like the snakes of black Tisiphone,
Sting me with their embracings. Mosby's arms
Shall compass me, and, were I made a star,
I would have none other spheres but those.
There is no nectar but in Mosby's lips!
Had chaste Diana kissed him, she like me
Would grow love sick, and from her wat'ry bower
Fling down Endymion and snatch him up.
Then blame not me that slay a silly man
Not half so lovely as Endymion.

Here enters Michael

MICHAEL Mistress, my master is coming hard by.

ALICE Who comes with him?

MICHAEL Nobody but Mosby.

ALICE That's well, Michael. Fetch in the tables, and, when thou hast done, stand before the counting-house door.

MICHAEL Why so?

ALICE Black Will is locked within to do the deed.

MICHAEL What? Shall he die to night?

ALICE Ay, Michael.

MICHAEL But shall not Susan know it?

ALICE Yes, for she'll be as secret as ourselves.

MICHAEL That's brave! I'll go fetch the tables.

ALICE But, Michael, hark to me a word or two:
When my husband is come in, lock the street door;

14.140 **snakes...Tisiphone** In Greek mythology, Tisiphone was one of the three furies (or avenging deities). Furies were often depicted with serpents interwoven with their hair.

14.143 **spheres** enclosure, i.e. Mosby's arms (alluding to the idea, in Ptolemaic astronomy, of a series of heavenly spheres surrounded the earth)

14.145–7 **Diana...snatch him up** In Greek mythology, Diana fell so fervently in love with Endymion, a beautiful mortal man, that she descended from her *wat'ry bower* (the moon) every night to embrace him as he slept.

14.148 **man** i.e. Arden

14.149 **Endymion** i.e. Mosby

14.153 **tables** dice board

He shall he be murdered ere the guests come in. *Exit Michael*

Here enter Arden and Mosby

Husband, what mean you to bring Mosby home?
Although I wished you to be reconciled,
'Twas more for fear of you than love of him.
Black Will and Greene are his companïons,
And they are cutters and may cut you short.
Therefore I thought it good to make you friends.
But wherefore do you bring him hither now?
You have given me my supper with his sight.

MOSBY Master Arden, methinks your wife would have me gone.

ARDEN No, good Master Mosby, women will be prating.
Alice, bid him welcome; he and I are friends.

ALICE You may enforce me to it if you will,
But I had rather die than bid him welcome.
His company hath purchased me ill friends,
And therefore will I ne'er frequent it more.

MOSBY [*aside*] O, how cunningly she can dissemble!

ARDEN [*to Alice*] Now he is here, you will not serve me so.

ALICE I pray you, be not angry or displeased.
I'll bid him welcome, seeing you'll have it so.—
You are welcome, Master Mosby. Will you sit down?

[*Then Mosby sits in the chair*]

MOSBY I know I am welcome to your loving husband,
But for yourself, you speak not from your heart.

ALICE And if I do not, sir, think I have cause.

MOSBY Pardon me, Master Arden, I'll away.

ARDEN No, good Master Mosby.

ALICE [*to Mosby*] We shall have guests enough though you go hence.

MOSBY I pray you, Master Arden, let me go.

ARDEN I pray thee, Mosby, let her prate her fill.

ALICE The doors are open, sir, you may be gone.

14.167 **of you** for you
14.172 **given me my supper** made me lose my appetite, as though I had already eaten (but also 'given me Mosby, who satisfies my appetites')
14.174 **prating** talking idly, foolishly
14.180 **dissemble** i.e. disguise herself, act

MICHAEL [*aside*] Nay, that's a lie, for I have locked the doors.

ARDEN [*to Michael*] Sirrah, fetch me a cup of wine. I'll make them friends. [*Exit Michael*]
And gentle Mistress Alice, seeing you are so stout,
You shall begin. Frown not; I'll have it so.

ALICE I pray you, meddle with that you have to do.

ARDEN Why, Alice, how can I do too much for him,
Whose life I have endangered without cause?

[*Enter Michael with wine*]

ALICE 'Tis true, and, seeing 'twas partly through my means,
I am content to drink to him for this once.
Here, Master Mosby!

[*Then she drinks to him*]

And, I pray you, henceforth
Be you as strange to me as I to you.
Your company hath purchased me ill friends,
And I for you, God knows, have undeservèd
Been ill spoken of in every place;
Therefore henceforth frequent my house no more.

MOSBY I'll see your husband in despite of you.
Yet Arden, I protest to thee by heaven,
Thou ne'er shalt see me more after this night.
I'll go to Rome rather than be forsworn.

ARDEN Tush, I'll have no such vows made in my house.

ALICE Yes, I pray you, husband, let him swear.—
And on that condition, Mosby, pledge me here.

MOSBY Ay, as willingly as I mean to live.

[*Then Alice hands him the cup, and he drinks to her*]

ARDEN Come, Alice, is our supper ready yet?

ALICE It will by then you have played a game at tables.

[*Then Arden sits on a stool*]

ARDEN Come, Master Mosby, what shall we play for?

14.196 **stout** stubborn
14.206 **undeservèd** undeservedly
14.212 **I'll...forsworn** I would rather become a Catholic than lie (about you never seeing me again)
14.218 **It will by then** it will be ready by the time

MOSBY Three games for a French crown, sir, an't please you.

ARDEN Content.

Then they play at the tables

[*Here enter Will and Shakebag from the counting-house*]

WILL [*aside to Alice*] Can he not take him yet? What a spite is that!

ALICE [*aside to Will*] Not yet, Will. Take heed he see thee not!

WILL [*aside to Alice*] I fear he will spy me as I am coming.

MICHAEL [*aside to Will*] To prevent that, creep betwixt my legs.

MOSBY [*to Arden*] One ace, or else I lose the game.

[*Then he throws the dice*]

ARDEN Marry, sir, there's two, for failing.

MOSBY Ah, Master Arden, 'Now I can take you!'

Then Will pulls him down with a towel

ARDEN Mosby! Michael! Alice! What will you do?

WILL Nothing but take you up, sir, nothing else.

[*Then Mosby stabs Arden*]

MOSBY There's for the pressing-iron you told me of.

[*Then Shakebag stabs Arden*]

SHAKEBAG And there's for the ten pound in my sleeve.

ALICE [*to Arden*] What, groans thou?
[*To Mosby*] Nay then, give me the weapon!—
Take this for hind'ring Mosby's love and mine.

[*Then Alice stabs Arden and he dies*]

MICHAEL O, mistress!

WILL Ah, that villain will betray us all.

MOSBY Tush, fear him not: he will be secret.

MICHAEL Why, dost thou think I will betray myself?

SHAKEBAG In Southwark dwells a bonny northern lass,

14.222 **spite** outrage

14.226 **One ace** i.e. roll a one. The ace is the side of the dice marked with a single dot.

14.230 **take you up** attack you

14.231 **There's…of** See 1.311.

14.239 **Southwark** A borough south of the Thames, formerly independent of the London city government, Southwark was a site for playhouses and brothels.

14.239 **bonny** pretty

The widow Chambley; I'll to her house now,
And if she will not give me harborough
I'll make booty of the quean, even to her smock.

WILL Shift for yourselves; we two will leave you now.

ALICE First lay the body in the counting-house.

Then they lay the body in the counting-house

WILL We have our gold. Mistress Alice, adieu.
Mosby, farewell—and Michael, farewell too.

Exeunt [*Will and Shakebag*]

[*Then knocking, and*] *enter Susan*

SUSAN Mistress, the guests are at the doors.
Hearken! They knock. What, shall I let them in?

ALICE Mosby, go thou and bear them company. *Exit Mosby*
And Susan, fetch water and wash away this blood.

[*Then Susan fetches water and washes the floor*]

SUSAN The blood cleaveth to the ground and will not out.

ALICE But with my nails I'll scrape away the blood.

[*Then she scrapes the floor*]

The more I strive, the more the blood appears!

SUSAN What's the reason, mistress, can you tell?

ALICE Because I blush not at my husband's death.

Here enters Mosby

MOSBY How now, what's the matter? Is all well?

ALICE Ay, well, if Arden were alive again.
In vain we strive, for here his blood remains.

MOSBY Why, strew rushes on it, can you not?
This wench doth nothing! [*To Susan*] Fall unto the work!

ALICE 'Twas thou that made me murder him.

MOSBY What of that?

ALICE Nay, nothing, Mosby, so it be not known.

MOSBY Keep thou it close, and 'tis unpossible.

14.241 **harborough** harbour, shelter
14.242 **quean** strumpet
14.242 **smock** undergarment
14.243 **Shift** fare
14.248 **Hearken** listen
14.259 **rushes** (customarily strewn on the floor in Elizabethan houses)
14.263 **close** secret

ALICE Ah, but I cannot. Was he not slain by me?
My husband's death torments me at the heart.

MOSBY It shall not long torment thee, gentle Alice.
I am thy husband: think no more of him.

Here enter Adam Fowle and Bradshaw

BRADSHAW How now, Mistress Arden? What ail you weep?

MOSBY Because her husband is abroad so late.
A couple of ruffians threatened him yesternight,
And she, poor soul, is afraid he should be hurt.

ADAM Is't nothing else? Tush, he'll be here anon.

Here enters Greene

GREENE Now, Mistress Arden, lack you any guests?

ALICE Ah, Master Greene, did you see my husband lately?

GREENE I saw him walking behind the Abbey even now.

Here enters Franklin

ALICE I do not like this being out so late.
Master Franklin, where did you leave my husband?

FRANKLIN Believe me, I saw him not since morning.
Fear you not: he'll come anon. Meantime,
You may do well to bid his guests sit down.

ALICE Ay, so they shall. Master Bradshaw, sit you there.
I pray you be content, I'll have my will.
Master Mosby, sit you in my husband's seat.

[*Then the guests sit down, and Susan and Michael whisper*]

MICHAEL Susan, shall thou and I wait on them? Or, an thou say'st the word, let us sit down too.

SUSAN Peace, we have other matters now in hand.
I fear me, Michael, all will be bewrayed.

MICHAEL Tush, so it be known that I shall marry thee in the morning, I care not though I be hanged ere night.
But to prevent the worst, I'll buy some ratsbane.

SUSAN Why, Michael, wilt thou poison thyself?

14.268 **What...weep** i.e. what ills are making you weep?
14.269 **abroad** out in public
14.287 **bewrayed** betrayed, disclosed
14.290 **ratsbane** rat-poison

MICHAEL No, but my mistress, for I fear she'll tell.
SUSAN Tush, Michael, fear not her; she's wise enough.
MOSBY Sirrah Michael, give's a cup of beer.
[*Then Michael gives him a cup*]
Mistress Arden, here's to your husband.
[*Then Mosby drinks*]
ALICE My husband?
FRANKLIN What ails you, woman, to cry so suddenly?
ALICE Ah, neighbours, a sudden qualm came over my heart.
My husband's being forth torments my mind.
I know something's amiss. He is not well,
Or else I should have heard of him ere now.
MOSBY [*aside*] She will undo us through her foolishness.
GREENE Fear not, Mistress Arden, he's well enough.
ALICE Tell not me; I know he is not well.
He was not wont for to stay thus late.—
Good Master Franklin, go and seek him forth,
And, if you find him, send him home to me,
And tell him what a fear he hath put me in.
FRANKLIN I like not this; I pray God all be well.
I'll seek him out, and find him if I can.
Exeunt Franklin, Mosby, and Greene
ALICE [*aside to Michael*] Michael, how shall I do to rid the rest away?
MICHAEL [*aside to Alice*] Leave that to my charge; let me alone.—
'Tis very late, Master Bradshaw, and there are many false knaves abroad,
And you have many narrow lanes to pass.
BRADSHAW Faith, friend Michael, and thou sayest true.
Therefore I pray thee light's forth, and lend's a link.
ALICE Michael, bring them to the doors, but do not stay;
You know I do not love to be alone.
Exeunt Bradshaw, Adam, and Michael
Go, Susan, and bid thy brother come.

14.294 **give's** give us
14.315 **narrow lanes** i.e. alleys
14.317 **link** torch

But wherefore should he come? Here is nought but fear.
Stay, Susan, stay, and help to counsel me.

SUSAN Alas! I, counsel? Fear frights away my wits.

Then they open the counting-house door and look upon Arden

ALICE See, Susan, where thy *quondam* master lies:
Sweet Arden, smeared in blood and filthy gore.

SUSAN My brother, you and I shall rue this deed.

ALICE Come, Susan, help to lift his body forth,
And let our salt tears be his obsequies.

[*Then they bring his body from the counting-house*]

Here enter Mosby and Greene

MOSBY How now, Alice! Whither will you bear him?

ALICE Sweet Mosby, art thou come? Then weep that will.
I have my wish in that I 'joy thy sight.

GREENE Well, it 'hoves us to be circumspect.

MOSBY Ay, for Franklin thinks that we have murdered him.

ALICE Ay, but he cannot prove it for his life.
We'll spend this night in dalliance and in sport.

Here enters Michael

MICHAEL O mistress, the Mayor and all the watch
Are coming towards our house with glaives and bills.

ALICE Make the door fast! Let them not come in.

[*Then Michael locks the street door*]

MOSBY Tell me, sweet Alice, how shall I escape?

ALICE Out at the back door, over the pile of wood,
And for one night lie at the Flower-de-Luce.

MOSBY That is the next way to betray myself.

GREENE Alas, Mistress Arden! The watch will take me here
And cause suspicion, where else would be none.

ALICE Why, take that way that Master Mosby doth—

14.324 **quondam** former (Latin)
14.328 **obsequies** funerary rites (usually in the form of commemorative lament)
14.331 **'joy** enjoy
14.332 **'hoves** behooves
14.335 **dalliance** frivolous activity
14.335 **sport** entertainment, amusement
14.337 **glaives and bills** broadswords and halberds (two-handed pole weapons topped with a blade)

But first convey the body to the fields.

Then they bear the body [*through the door*] *into the fields*

MOSBY Until tomorrow, sweet Alice, now farewell,
And see you cònfess nothing in any case.

GREENE Be resolute, Mistress Alice; betray us not,
But cleave to us as we will stick to you. *Exeunt Mosby and Greene*

ALICE Now let the judge and juries do their worst;
My house is clear, and now I fear them not.

[*Here enter Susan and Michael*]

SUSAN As we went, it snowèd all the way,
Which makes me fear our footsteps will be spied.

ALICE Peace, fool! The snow will cover them again.

SUSAN But it had done before we came back again.

[*Then there is knocking at the door*]

ALICE Hark, hark, they knock! Go, Michael, let them in.

[*Then Michael opens the door*]

Here enter the Mayor and the Watch

How now, Master Mayor, have you brought my husband home?

MAYOR I saw him come into your house an hour ago.

ALICE You are deceived: it was a Londoner.

MAYOR Mistress Arden, know you not one that is called Black Will?

ALICE I know none such. What mean these questïons?

MAYOR I have the Council's warrant to apprehend him.

ALICE [*aside*] I am glad it is no worse.
Why, Master Mayor, think you I harbour any such?

MAYOR We are informed that here he is—
And therefore pardon us, for we must search.

ALICE Ay, search and spare you not, through every room.
Were my husband at home, you would not offer this.

[*Then the Mayor and the Watch begin to search*]

Here enters Franklin

Master Franklin, what mean you come so sad?

14.350 **cleave** adhere

FRANKLIN Arden, thy husband and my friend, is slain.
ALICE Ah, by whom? Master Franklin, can you tell?
FRANKLIN I know not, but behind the Abbey
There he lies murdered in most piteous case.
MAYOR But Master Franklin, are you sure 'tis he?
FRANKLIN I am too sure. Would God I were deceived!
ALICE Find out the murd'rers! Let them be known.
FRANKLIN Ay, so they shall. Come you along with us.
ALICE Wherefore?
FRANKLIN Know you this hand-towel and this knife?
SUSAN [*aside*] Ah Michael, through this thy negligence thou hast betrayed and undone us all.
MICHAEL [*aside*] I was so afraid I knew not what I did. I thought I had thrown them both into the well.
ALICE [*to Franklin*] It is the pig's blood we had to supper.
But wherefore stay you? Find out the murd'rers.
MAYOR I fear me you'll prove one of them yourself.
ALICE I, one of them? What mean such questïons?
FRANKLIN [*to Mayor*] I fear me he was murdered in this house
And carried to the fields, for from that place
Backwards and forwards may you see
The print of many feet within the snow.
And look about this chamber where we are,
And you shall find part of his guiltless blood;
For in his slip-shoe did I find some rushes,
Which argueth he was murdered in this room.
MAYOR [*to Watch*] Look in the place where he was wont to sit.
See, see! His blood! It is too manifest.
ALICE It is a cup of wine that Michael shed.
MICHAEL Ay, truly.
FRANKLIN It is his blood, which, strumpet, thou hast shed.
But, if I live, thou and thy complices,
Which have conspired and wrought his death, shall rue it.

14.374 **piteous case** in a most distressing manner
14.395 **slip-shoe** slipper
14.402 **complices** accomplices
14.403 **wrought** fashioned

ALICE Ah, Master Franklin, God and heaven can tell
I loved him more than all the world beside.
But bring me to him; let me see his body.

[*Then Franklin points to Michael and Susan*]

FRANKLIN [*to Watch*] Bring that villain, and Mosby's sister too—
And one of you go to the Flower-de-Luce
And seek for Mosby, and apprehend him too. *Exeunt*

Sc. 15

Here enters Shakebag solus

SHAKEBAG The widow Chambly in her husband's days I kept,
And, now he's dead, she is grown so stout
She will not know her old companïons.
I came thither, thinking to have had
Harbour, as I was wont,
And she was ready to thrust me out at doors.
But whether she would or no, I got me up—
And as she followed me, I spurned her down the stairs,
And broke her neck, and cut her tapster's throat;
And now I am going to fling them in the Thames.
I have the gold; what care I though it be known?
I'll cross the water and take sanctuary. *Exit Shakebag*

Sc. 16

Here enter the Mayor, [*and the Watch, guarding*] *Mosby, Alice, Franklin, Michael, and Susan*

MAYOR See, Mistress Arden, where your husband lies.

[*Then he reveals the body*]

Confess this foul fault, and be penitent.

ALICE Arden, sweet husband, what shall I say?
The more I sound his name, the more he bleeds.

Sc. 15 15.1 **kept** i.e. as a paramour
15.2 **stout** proud
15.8 **spurned** kicked

Sc. 16 16.4–6 **The more . . . did it** (refers to the popular superstition that the corpse of a murder victim bled in the presence of the murderer)

This blood condemns me, and in gushing forth
Speaks as it falls and asks me why I did it.
Forgive me, Arden. I repent me now,
And, would my death save thine, thou shouldst not die.
Rise up, sweet Arden, and enjoy thy love,
And frown not on me when we meet in heaven.
In heaven I love thee, though on earth I did not.

MAYOR Say, Mosby, what made thee murder him?

FRANKLIN [*to Mosby*] Study not for an answer; look not down.
His purse and girdle found at thy bed's head
Witness sufficiently thou didst the deed.
It bootless is to swear thou didst it not.

MOSBY I hired Black Will and Shakebag, ruffians both,
And they and I have done this murd'rous deed.
But wherefore stay we? Come and bear me hence.

FRANKLIN Those ruffians shall not escape. I will up to London,
And get the Council's warrant to apprehend them. *Exeunt*

Sc. 17

Here enters Will

WILL Shakebag, I hear, hath taken sanctuary,
But I am so pursued with hues and cries
For petty robberies that I have done
That I can come unto no sanctuary.
Therefore must I, in some oyster-boat,
At last be fain to go aboard some hoy,
And so to Flushing. There is no staying here.
At Sittingbourne the watch was like to take me—
And, had I not with my buckler covered my head,
And run full blank at all adventures,

16.13 **Study not** i.e. do not try to fabricate
16.14 **girdle** belt
16.16 **bootless** useless

Sc. 17 17.6 **hoy** small boat
17.7 **Flushing** modern Vlissingen, a major port in the Netherlands; but also a coastal village in Cornwall. (Historically, Black Will first fled to Cornwall, then later to Vlissingen.)
17.10 **full...adventures** i.e. proceeding without regard to the consequences of my actions

I am sure I had ne'er gone further than that place,
For the constable had twenty warrants to apprehend me.
Besides that, I robbed him and his man once at Gads Hill.
Farewell, England; I'll to Flushing now. *Exit Will*

Sc. 18

Here enter the Mayor, [*and the Watch, guarding*] *Mosby, Alice, Michael, Susan, and Bradshaw*

MAYOR [*to Watch*] Come, make haste, and bring away the prisoners.

BRADSHAW Mistress Arden, you are now going to God,
And I am by the law condemned to die
About a letter I brought from Master Greene.
I pray you, Mistress Arden, speak the truth:
Was I ever privy to your intent, or no?

ALICE What should I say? You brought me such a letter.
But I dare swear thou knewest not the contents.
Leave now to trouble me with worldly things,
And let me meditate upon my saviour Christ,
Whose blood must save me for the blood I shed.

MOSBY How long shall I live in this hell of grief?
Convey me from the presence of that strumpet.

ALICE Ah, but for thee I had never been strumpet.
What cannot oaths and protestations do
When men have opportunity to woo?
I was too young to sound thy villainies;
But now I find it, and repent too late.

SUSAN [*to Mosby*] Ah, gentle brother, wherefore should I die?
I knew not of it till the deed was done.

MOSBY For thee I mourn more than for myself.
But let it suffice. I cannot save thee now.

MICHAEL An if your brother and my mistress had not promised me you in marriage, I had ne'er given consent to this foul deed.

17.13 **Gads Hill** (hill on the road from London to Rochester, notorious for robberies)

Sc. 18 18.4 **About** because of
18.6 **privy** aware
18.9 **Leave** cease
18.17 **sound** measure

MAYOR Leave to accuse each other now,
And listen to the sentence I shall give.
Bear Mosby and his sister to London straight,
Where they in Smithfield must be executed.
Bear Mistress Arden unto Canterbury,
Where her sentence is she must be burnt.
Michael and Bradshaw in Faversham must suffer death.

ALICE Let my death make amends for all my sins.

MOSBY Fie upon women!—This shall be my song.
But bear me hence, for I have lived too long.

SUSAN Seeing no hope on earth, in heaven is my hope.

MICHAEL Faith, I care not, seeing I die with Susan.

BRADSHAW My blood be on his head that gave the sentence!

MAYOR To speedy execution with them all. *Exeunt*

Epilogue

Here enters Franklin

FRANKLIN Thus have you seen the truth of Arden's death.
As for the ruffians, Shakebag and Black Will,
The one took sanctuary and, being sent for out,
Was murderèd in Southwark, as he passed
To Greenwich, where the Lord Protector lay.
Black Will was burnt in Flushing on a stage.
Greene was hanged at Osbridge in Kent.
The painter fled, and how he died we know not.
But this above the rest is to be noted:
Arden lay murdered in that plot of ground
Which he by force and violence held from Reede,
And in the grass his body's print was seen
Two years and more after the deed was done.
Gentlemen, we hope you'll pardon this naked tragedy

18.28 **Smithfield** (an open space, northwest of the Tower of London, just outside the city walls; thieves were often executed there)

Epi.6 **stage** scaffold

Epi.7 **Osbridge** (a village close to Faversham)

Epi.14 **naked** plain in style, hiding nothing. (Truth was proverbially naked.)

Wherein no filèd points are foisted in
To make it gracious to the ear or eye;
For simple truth is gracïous enough
And needs no other points of glozing stuff. [*Exit*]

Epi.15 **filèd points** stylistic ornament (i.e. rhetorical figures)

Epi.15 **foisted** unnecessarily imposed

Epi.18 **glozing stuff** specious padding or stuffing

The Oxford World's Classics Website

www.oxfordworldsclassics.com

- Browse the full range of Oxford World's Classics online
- Sign up for our monthly e-alert to receive information on new titles
- Read extracts from the Introductions
- Listen to our editors and translators talk about the world's greatest literature with our Oxford World's Classics audio guides
- Join the conversation, follow us on Twitter at OWC_Oxford
- Teachers and lecturers can order inspection copies quickly and simply via our website

www.oxfordworldsclassics.com

MORE ABOUT **OXFORD WORLD'S CLASSICS**

American Literature

British and Irish Literature

Children's Literature

Classics and Ancient Literature

Colonial Literature

Eastern Literature

European Literature

Gothic Literature

History

Medieval Literature

Oxford English Drama

Philosophy

Poetry

Politics

Religion

The Oxford Shakespeare

A SELECTION OF **OXFORD WORLD'S CLASSICS**

	An Anthology of Elizabethan Prose Fiction
	Early Modern Women's Writing
	Three Early Modern Utopias (Utopia; New Atlantis; The Isle of Pines)
Francis Bacon	Essays The Major Works
Aphra Behn	Oroonoko and Other Writings The Rover and Other Plays
John Bunyan	Grace Abounding The Pilgrim's Progress
John Donne	The Major Works Selected Poetry
John Foxe	Book of Martyrs
Ben Jonson	The Alchemist and Other Plays The Devil is an Ass and Other Plays Five Plays
John Milton	The Major Works Paradise Lost Selected Poetry
Earl of Rochester	Selected Poems
Sir Philip Sidney	The Old Arcadia The Major Works
Sir Philip and Mary Sidney	The Sidney Psalter
Izaak Walton	The Compleat Angler

A SELECTION OF **OXFORD WORLD'S CLASSICS**

	The Anglo-Saxon World
	Beowulf
	Lancelot of the Lake
	The Paston Letters
	Sir Gawain and the Green Knight
	The Poetic Edda
	The Mabinogion
	Tales of the Elders of Ireland
	York Mystery Plays
GEOFFREY CHAUCER	The Canterbury Tales Troilus and Criseyde
GUILLAUME DE LORRIS and JEAN DE MEUN	The Romance of the Rose
HENRY OF HUNTINGDON	The History of the English People 1000–1154
JOCELIN OF BRAKELOND	Chronicle of the Abbey of Bury St Edmunds
WILLIAM LANGLAND	Piers Plowman
SIR JOHN MANDEVILLE	The Book of Marvels and Travels
SIR THOMAS MALORY	Le Morte Darthur